# Strandline

**Produced by**
Ron Nicola and Rosemary Bartholomew,
Hastings Writers' Group

**Artwork**
Cover image: Janet Tredinnick

*The following authors have also illustrated their own work:*
Ron Nicola *(Hopscotch, Beyond the Tempest)*
Jean Russell-Parnell *(Controlled Freak)*
John Vallender *(Runner Beans and Mint Sauce, Goodbye)*

*Additional illustrations*
Ron Nicola

Photograph of Coronation Clock Tower reproduced by kind permission of
Bexhill Library

All copyright © of both text and illustrations remains with the original authors
and artists.

All rights reserved. No part of this work may be reproduced or stored in an
information retrieval system (other than for purposes of review) without prior
written permission of the copyright holder.

A catalogue record of this book is available from the British Library.

First edition: December 2005

ISBN:1-84375-211-5

To order additional copies of this book please visit:
http://www.upso.co.uk/hastingswriters

Published by: UPSO Ltd
5 Stirling Road, Castleham Business Park,
St Leonards-on-Sea, East Sussex TN38 9NW UK
Tel: 01424 853349  Fax: 0870 191 3991
E-mail: info@upso.co.uk  Web: http//www.upso.co.uk

# Strandline

## Hastings Writers' Group

**UPSO**

# Foreword

Hastings Writers' Group is pleased to introduce *Strandline* Volume 5. Included is a creative selection of members' writing, reflecting versatile talents and wide-ranging interests. Every member, from beginner to professional, was invited to participate in this showcase of our work. We hope you will enjoy reading it as much as we have all enjoyed contributing.

It has been very encouraging that our previous two volumes of Strandline have won national awards. Volume 4 won The National Association of Writers' Groups (NAWG) Denise Robertson Trophy for the best group anthology and Volume 3 won the David St John Thomas Charitable Trust anthology trophy.

In this latest volume we have also included the six prize-winning entries from our annual national short story competition, the *Legend Writing Award*. The winners were judged by our patron, award-winning author David Gemmell. His continued support and encouragement are much appreciated.

*Hastings Writers' Group*
*December 2005*

# Contents

| | | |
|---|---|---|
| Lover Come Back to Me | *Richard Wheeler* | 1 |
| Perfectly | *Ken Baker* | 5 |
| The Spirit is Willing | *Sue Whitehead* | 11 |
| Sisters | *Charlotte Praeger* | 12 |
| Think Rainbow | *Mary Rothwell* | 14 |
| Gabriel | *Monica Percy* | 19 |
| Reflections | *Janet Tredinnick* | 24 |
| The Home Décor Wars | *John Enefer* | 28 |
| Icarus Heart | *Richard Wheeler* | 30 |
| The Right Ear of Malchus | *Gwenda J Lee* | 31 |
| The Mission | *Michael Smith* | 37 |
| Poppies | *Linda Cunniffe* | 40 |
| No DSS! | *Tania Oriol* | 48 |
| Residential Friends | *Tania Oriol* | 50 |
| The River | *Sarah Chandler* | 51 |
| Hopscotch | *Ron Nicola* | 54 |
| Runner Beans & Mint Sauce | *John Vallender* | 59 |
| Spiritus Sancti | *Joe Strange* | 63 |
| Philosophy of Knowledge | *Joe Strange* | 64 |
| The Scorecard | *Richard Holdsworth* | 66 |
| *Controlled* Freak | *Jean Russell-Parnell* | 70 |
| A Photo on the Shelf | *Anne Hooker* | 74 |
| Coronation Clock Tower | *Paul Lendon* | 76 |
| Not Trying to Cause a Big S-Sensation | *Ken Baker* | 77 |

| | | |
|---|---|---|
| Castle in the Sea | *Tony Pook* | 80 |
| Yesterday and Today | *Mike Counsell* | 82 |
| At the Café Moon | *Mary Rothwell* | 84 |
| In Search of Andrew Young | *Kenneth Overend* | 85 |
| Goodbye | *John Vallender* | 88 |
| Morality | *Bill Burkitt* | 90 |
| The Last Train | *Ann Hubbard* | 91 |
| Lollipop | *John Stevens* | 92 |
| Happy Birthday | *Mike Counsell* | 95 |
| The Empty Canvas | *Linda Mooncie* | 102 |
| Bargain Christmas | *Linda Mooncie* | 104 |
| Childhood | *Linda Mooncie* | 105 |
| Vintage Beauties | *Tania Oriol* | 106 |
| Read On… | *Rosemary Bartholomew* | 109 |
| The Prize | *Anon* | 113 |
| Sydney Little: Visionary or Villain? | *Michael Smith* | 117 |
| For a Golfing Friend | *Ken Baker* | 120 |
| This | *Kenneth Overend* | 121 |
| Beyond the Tempest | *Ron Nicola* | 122 |
| Fighting Back | *Jean Russell-Parnell* | 124 |

**Legend Writing Award Prizewinners**

| | | |
|---|---|---|
| Eating Shrivelled Fruit | *Yvonne Jackson* | 133 |
| Under the Brim | *Anne Youngson* | 138 |
| A May Wedding | *Christine Buckland* | 142 |
| Thirty Different Words for Sand | *John Barfield* | 146 |
| Dead Leaves | *Alexandra Fox* | 152 |
| Where Ocean Meets Lagoon | *Monica Watson-Peck* | 156 |

# Lover Come Back to Me

Morpheus dreams;

I remember the smell of crushed grass and warm earth, and I remember the breeze caressing our bodies, making the fine down of your skin rise in peach smooth softness, but that was a long way from here, somewhere in the warmer days of our youth.

The darkness inside my eyelids isn't cold, there's a warm glow from the brilliance of the sun. I can feel its heat through the glass of the conservatory, caressing my skin as gently as I caressed yours. I followed the curve of your stomach as it rose and fell with each soft breath of summer air, and I traced the outline of your breast against the pale blue of the sky as I lay beside you. You shuddered as my fingertip grazed slowly across the softness of your nipple and I stopped, half afraid that you had found my touch repulsive, then you stretched, arching your back. You reached out, pulled me closer, until our lips met.

The scents of the garden play gentle games with my nose, carrying with them elusive memories on the almost imperceptible zephyrs of the breeze, and I remember the other scents of that far away time. You wore apple blossom and its soft fragrance lingered, even over the musky smell of our love.

I can hear you, the sound of your trowel scraping past grit and stones as it slices through the soil, and I remember the smell of cool earth after rain. The sound of water dripping through the leaves as we sheltered from a summer storm. Your thin dress soaked through, so that it clung to your body. The wetness made the buttons difficult to undo. There was something sensual in the contrast between the softness of your skin and the mossy roughness of the bark as you pulled me into you. You laughed as the drips exploded on your skin, each one a burst of coolness in the heat of our love, and with each fresh drop you tried to pull me deeper into your warmth.

Morpheus dreams and darkness enfolds;

The sharp tinkle of a teaspoon briskly stirring one spoonful into the brown depths of the cup. That first tentative sip of hot tea, expectant, waiting for the tannic ripeness to roll across the taste buds. How I remember the taste of you, salt and bitter-sweet in that hot summer field. The corn waving ripe golden ears at the cotton wool clouds in the sky. Was that when you became ripe too? Swelling gently into the winter and giving birth in the promise of spring. That seems so long ago, now that our birds have flown their nest.

My tongue feels dry and sticky. What wouldn't I give for a good old-fashioned cup of tea? Not tea bags, real tea. Tea you can smell when you open the packet. I wonder if, when I open my eyes, there will be a cup, but no, there will only be a glass of tepid water and a straw. I won't drink from one of those blasted feeder cups, the ones with the lid on. Disgusting plastic things. People would think I've run into my second childhood, but you know that isn't true. I want tea, a real cup of tea!

Morpheus waves a tender hand;

Have you noticed how the sun moves more quickly these days? It seems only a moment ago that it was straight ahead, high over the trees at the bottom of the garden, and now it's quite far over to the right. It's still warm, but my feet are cold, it's almost as though they're in a bowl of cold water.

Now there's a thing I'd almost forgotten, do you remember skinny dipping in the river? It seemed such a romantic thing to do. You were a picture in the moonlight, Venus rising from the waters. I remember afterwards, laying on the riverbank with you astride me, cold water dripping from your hair as you rocked gently back and forth. We were covered in mud from head to foot, how did we ever get home without being noticed? I remember all the mosquito bites we had afterwards too; we must have used so much calamine lotion.

Arising from the arms of Morpheus I wake, but there is no tea, there is no you, there is only this tepid water and the straw and the fading afternoon. The chill has risen to my knees and the blanket, wrapped tight and tucked professionally in, feels coarse under my fingers. Age is no friend to be welcomed, when along with wisdom it brings dissolution and corruption. Sight fades, and sound becomes a distant rumble. A blessing against the stuff they call music now. If only I couldn't hear them remind me that you're not here. They think I'm losing it, they think the old grey matter's turning gooey, but it's not. I know what's going on, and I know where you are. I know where I am too, and where I'm going, but knowing doesn't mean that I have to like it, and I don't have to think about it either.

Taste buds fail you know? Food, once such a pleasure, has become a bland, grey, spoon-fed thing, and the world has become bland and grey with it. I can still smell though. Night scented stocks are my favourite. Their heady perfume brings you back to me for a fleeting moment.

I'll do without the tea and drink a little water. It tastes tepid and dead, and the glass slips in my fingers. It bounces because it's plastic and for once I wish it was glass, I wish I could hear the clear ringing sound of breaking glass and the tears begin to fall as the water spreads in an incontinent pool on the tiled floor, and you are there at my side, dressed all in white, only it isn't you. Your voice was stilled in death long ago while mine lingered on railing against the Gods who took you, all too soon, for their own.

The pool is mopped up and there is water in the hateful, modern, plastic glass, but I can't be bothered to try and pick it up again. If I drop it they'll come back, reminding me that you aren't here, you've gone.

The whir of the pump is comforting, to hear it push a little more pain-relieving liquid into my veins brings a kind of peace, and with it comes another step closer to that final relief from which there is no waking.

Once more into the arms of dear Morpheus I fall.

If I open my eyes I can see the fires of the sunset setting the wisps of cloud aflame, but it reminds me of the night we stood up on the Downs and watched London burn. After that I saw so many places burn and I was glad that you were at home, safe in the countryside with our children. It's strange, the way that the blue sky turns to green in some places, just before the fires go out and the stars return to guide us through the night, if it isn't raining, that is, and it always seems to be raining since you went away, but it isn't tonight and I wonder if you'll come back to me.

In a moment the nurse will come to wheel me back into the house but I'll argue. I'll tell her that I've got my blanket, and that I can't eat much anyway. I'll say I'm not hungry and I want to stay here, and that I'm old and so I ought to be allowed to do what I want to do because I'm old enough to look after myself, only I shan't say that last bit because I may be old enough, but I'm too ill and I can't, and she'll remind me that I can't and she'll tell me it's for my own good and wheel me inside anyway.

I won. She said it was a warm night and if I really didn't feel like eating I could stay out here for a little longer. I didn't tell her I was getting colder because she'd have taken me inside and I want to stay out here and wait for you. I'm sure you'll come back tonight. You always loved the stars, you called them your favourite blanket. You said the moon was your bedside lamp.

I remember later, not long before you went away, laying out on the Downs with you, watching the stars, and I wished that we could stay forever, but it didn't work. Maybe if I wish on one tonight you'll come back. I wish on that bright one straight ahead, and the pump makes its little noise.

I swear I can taste the stuff that it pumps into me you know. They say I can't, but how do they know?

My hands are getting cold, they're tucked into the blanket, but I can hardly feel them all the same. I suppose I should call someone, but I want to stay here, I don't want to go in. I'm not shivering so I can't be that cold, can I? Anyway, if I let them take me in I might miss you, and I so long to see you again. I want to hold you, to feel the warmth of your body close to mine, but all I can feel is the heat of the tears that are running down my cheeks, and the coldness that enfolds my limbs, but I'll wait a little longer, there's still time for you to come.

The coldness grows closer, but it doesn't hurt. In a strange way it feels quite warm. Warm and soft and drawing, so that all I want to do is settle into it and close my eyes, but if I close my eyes I might miss you, so I'll just hold on for a moment longer, then I'll blink and that way I won't miss you. The pump makes its noise again, and I blink a long blink and remember sitting beside you while you slept, trying not to blink in case I missed a precious moment.

And now I want to sleep, it draws me inwards and I can't stop my eyes closing. I call for help, but no sound breaks the silence and I can no longer move. All I can do is stay still and not breathe, and not feel the constant pain that has lived beside me for the last few years. The pain that became a friend because it stopped me thinking of the pain that lived with me after you went away, and now it is gone and there is no pain and I am going away too. Not breathing, yet feeling safe and warm, and free. With an easy grace I stand and turn, and you are there, standing behind the me that I once was, silently reaching out to embrace me in your warmth.

You have come back to me.

*Richard Wheeler*

# Perfectly

It was her attitude to the postcard that did it.

She has to go.

I picked it up from the hearth where she'd casually tossed it, intending for it to go on the fire of course. I read it again.

*Dear Dimitri,*

*This island is a terrible place. The guards here are inhuman, no mercy whatsoever. Yesterday they beat Carruthers senseless for eating a dead mouse. He's now just a shell of a man. It's my turn next but they won't get anything out of me. Tell everyone at Station Z that I'm thinking of them – it's lights out now – the nights are the worst, only the rats for company, they're gnawing away somewhere under my filthy mattress – hope this reaches you...*

*Father Julius*

What was her reaction when she read it? She snorted, that's what. Then she humphed in that really annoying way she has developed. That together with the look of bored pity.

'Oh I see,' she said, snorting, humphing and shaking her head. 'So it's from the Isle of Wight is it? So that's the "terrible place" is it? Well, I must say it looks *perfectly* all right to me.'

That was another thing. She'd got into the habit of using the word "perfectly" all the time, particularly when she was being sarcastic. Sometimes I would tick off on my fingers the number of times she used it. I could see she was about to go into one of her tirades so there wasn't much to do except wait it out.

'When are you two going to grow up? I know *perfectly* well Father Julius is actually your silly mate Dave, so when are you both going to stop pretending you're spies? Don't you know you're being *perfectly* ridiculous?'

Typical. What does she know anyway? Surely that's the whole point of being a spy? Nobody knows for certain who's a spy and who isn't, not even close members of a family. An uncle, a cousin or an aunt might look like ordinary people on the outside; they could be accountants, solicitors, bus drivers, but who knows? Who knows what secret lives they might be leading? She can sneer all she wants and of course she's perfectly entitled to do so. Did I really just say *perfectly*? It must be catching. But what does she know really?

Granted the postcard might have been more convincing without the scenic views of Cowes, Ventnor and the Needles. And Dave could try disguising his handwriting. What does it matter anyway? It's not just her constant doubting, it's lots of other things too.

Like the tea.

She knows I have a weakness for real tea, proper tea, in particular lapsang souchong. It's a waste of time ever asking her to put it on her shopping list, so a week or two ago I found a specialist tea shop in town and bought my own little packet of the fragrant leaves.

Getting home well before she was due I dug out the old brown teapot from the bottom of a kitchen cupboard. Then I thoroughly spoiled myself with the tea-making ceremony. I boiled the kettle, splashed in some hot water and swirled it round in the pot to warm it first. Next a carefully measured teaspoonful of the dark leaves. For good measure I added an extra one for the pot. I poured in the boiling water and replaced the lid without stirring, leaving the teapot to "stand" a full five minutes while I hunted for the strainer. I unlocked the glass cabinet and took out one of our hallowed, best china cups and matching saucer. When I judged a full five minutes had elapsed I poured the tea very slowly, inhaling the subtle aroma before adding a little dash of milk. I'd almost forgotten how wonderful tea could taste. I let the warm liquid float over my tongue and caress my throat before swallowing.

Exquisite.

I sat at the kitchen table for some time, enjoying the second cup possibly even more than the first. Sheer contentment. Amazing how much pleasure can be derived from a good cup of proper tea. To hell with silly tea bags full of nothing but dust. Right then the world, or rather my little part of it, seemed a lovely place.

Then suddenly it wasn't.

I didn't hear her come in. It wasn't until the kitchen door burst open that I realised she was home. She thumped two Tesco shopping bags on the work surface and began to humph. Then she sniffed.

'What's that awful smell? What's that you've got? What's that teapot doing there? Why are you using our best china? You've made some of that horrible tea you like haven't you?'

She was the only person I knew who could ask and answer her own questions, usually in the same sentence. I smiled and tried to explain but there was no stopping her in mid-flow. She was a juggernaut once she got started.

'And I suppose you think you're going to pour all those tea leaves down my kitchen sink and then the drain will get blocked and then we'll have to get a plumber because it's no use asking you to try to unblock a drain. You wouldn't know where to start would you?'

She even wagged her finger at me. She could predict disasters long before they ever happened. A rare talent. Not wanting to argue and spoil my own mood I took the easy way out and, picking up the teapot, I went to the garden. Tealeaves were good for the roses weren't they? Anything to keep the peace.

I could have put up with her moaning but it didn't really stop there. A few days later I couldn't find the tea. She'd hidden it or thrown it away so I bought another packet. I wasn't going to give in but it was very irritating. Then she hid the tea strainer. This caught me by surprise so I decided to buy a spare and keep it in my briefcase. She'd never look in there. What would I do if she hid the teapot? Why was I playing this silly game, putting up with this nonsense? By now I'd decided.

Yes, I had.

She's got to go.


A few days later I was about to leave for the office when another postcard arrived on the doormat. This time she got there first. She came into the kitchen reading it out in her usual sneering manner.

*Red Leader, Red Leader,*

*Mayday Mayday Mayday. Port engine's on fire. Starboard's gone for a Burton too. Sparks looks like he's had it — must have copped a Jerry bullet. Sorry - won't be back in Blighty tonight but it's my round so all you chaps have a drink on me. Can't hang around chatting. Am baling out now. Tally-ho. Good luck. Over and out.*

*F.J.*

'F.J. is it? Father Julius again? Or should I say your silly mate Dave? So now you're supposed to be wartime pilots or some such nonsense? And you're "Red Leader" are you? Last week he was a spy. Now he sends you a postcard from a burning plane does he? I suppose it doesn't matter the war was over some sixty years ago and you have risen up to the great heights of being the assistant manager of a furniture shop? Oh and by the way this one's from Harrogate. What's your silly mate doing up there, not that I really care?'

'Well it could be in code couldn't it?' I answered, not that she was looking for an answer. Her questions were nearly always rhetorical. But she hadn't finished yet.

'One thing I'm *perfectly* sure of is that you and your silly mate Dave are never going to grow up. Idiots, you two. Well I can't hang around all day with this nonsense. You know *perfectly* well,' (again the wagging finger) 'it's my coffee morning at Rita's.'

I started to ask 'Where did you put the teapot...?' but she'd already slammed the door. Talk about *my* silly mates. Rita and the other "girls" were probably the silliest bunch imaginable, always campaigning for something or other, then pestering the rest of the village about it.

Time for some planning.

The Sunday started as a beautiful spring morning and the weather forecast promised an even warmer afternoon. Breakfast over, I was draining my second cup of ordinary teabag tea when I decided to put things in motion.

'How about a picnic this afternoon?' I suggested as she stacked the plates in the dishwasher. If looks could kill. She gave me the bored pity expression and then lots of reasons why a picnic was such a terrible idea, extra work for her making sandwiches and of course I ought to know *perfectly* well that there were bound to be ants and the weather forecast was always wrong and so on and so on.

'But you always used to enjoy picnics before we were married.'

Twenty-three years ago and when she was about three stones lighter.

'Look I'll make the sandwiches and a nice thermos of tea and we can take the rest of those rock cakes you made, the ones you brought back from your coffee morning at Rita's.'

Not surprising she brought them back. Her rock cakes were aptly named.

Gradually she started to come round.

'Well so long as we're back in time for my programme I suppose it wouldn't do any harm.'

Her so-called "programme" was Coronation Street but she never used its title. It was always her "programme." When did she start to become so boring?

A few hours later I'd clingfilmed the sandwiches, made up a thermos of her ghastly tea and put everything, including the infamous rock cakes, into the old wicker picnic basket we'd had from years ago.

When we were happy.

We made our way to the field just outside the village and found one of our old favourite spots on the top of a hill where there was plenty of shade from a large oak. She inspected for ants before spreading the tartan rug. She didn't like the sun these days; it seemed to give her a permanent squint. We'd just about unclinged our first sandwich when there was a deep rumbling sound from somewhere below the hill. Of course the disturbance was my fault. Naturally it was my job to investigate. She wasn't going to move.

I walked past the oak to the edge of the steep hill. A cement mixer was just trundling away below and about two hundred yards in the distance some workmen were loading a van and laughing. Two bulldozers were standing idle near the wooden site hut. What a mess they'd made. Thousands of trees gone, great ugly brown scars over the fields. The long awaited by-pass, the one she and Rita and the rest of the "girls" had been campaigning for with cardboard placards outside the Town Hall. Well now they'd got their way. Personally I didn't mind a few lorries coming through the village.

I heard a rustle and there she was standing beside me peering over the hill. The cement was fresh below. There was no-one around. The cement looked deep; it was the steepest of hills and only the slightest of nudges....

She let out a muffled humph and I swear she wagged her finger at me as she went. The cement glugged and bubbled for a few seconds, then swallowed her completely and found its own level again. Well she wanted the by-pass and now she's really giving it her full support.

The next day I went to my office, through the entrance of the furniture store just off Whitehall, all the way to the door at the back. I waited for the security light to go green before opening it and smiled at the receptionist in the corridor beyond. She smiled back. She has a lovely smile. Divorced, I believe.

'Your codename sir?'

'Dimitri.'

'Thank you sir, there's a message for you from Father Julius at Harrogate'.

She handed me a yellow slip of paper which I'd have to decode.

Not Dave again. I'd already dealt with his two coded postcards. What was he panicking about now? Why can't my Field Operatives keep cooler heads?

The girl smiled at me again. She really does have nice eyes.

'Oh one more thing sir, I've arranged that appointment you asked for with the Head of Identities and Disappearances. Does four o'clock suit you?'

'*Perfectly.*'

*Ken Baker*

# The Spirit is Willing

I don't want to be seen reading Saga magazine
I don't want to walk down Memory Lane
What we did back then,
Do you remember when?
Living in the past is such a pain.

I'll put my mementoes in the drawer,
Forget what went before.
The past has packed its bags and gone away.
I'll try to be courageous -
Do something quite outrageous.
Concentrate on living for today.

I'd like to visit Thailand,
Go back-packing in Greek islands
And do some lotus-eating in the sun.
Learn to free-fall from a plane.
Maybe fall in love again.
Might even have a toy-boy just for fun.

But ...

My eyesight's getting dimmer.
I *really need* my zimmer.
Haven't got the energy to sin.
So I'll spare you the oration
Of my latest operation
If you'll light me another fag and pass the gin!

*Sue Whitehead*

# Sisters

'Come on, if you're coming!'
I still hear the rasp, the tut
in your voice, but the flicker
of choice was cold as a blade
stroking my skin. I ran
after you. The metal steps
of the footbridge clanged
and shivered as we skittered
down the other side to the rec.

On the swings
you pushed me
so high the butterflies
jumped in my throat,
but my lips were tight.
You eased yourself back
then curving forward
swung higher and higher,
till I thought you'd fly
over the bar
but you laughed and leapt
onto the grass, and I smelled the chains
on my hands.

It rained. I tried to keep up.
Do you remember crossing the stream,
the reek of wild garlic,
the slippery log?
It wobbled and I was stuck.
I watched you disappear,
through clumps of nettles,
space stretching out
around me, a muddy trickle
deep below. I hated you.
I didn't know
the distance between us
wouldn't always be so big.

***Charlotte Praeger***

# Think Rainbow

That evening Robert telephoned.

'About Wales?'

'Yes?'

'Don't you think it would be better if you came with me, by car?'

Better for whom, thought Susan, but she said, 'What about Gemma?'

'She's not invited. Anyway, she needs to rest. The baby's due in seven weeks.'

Why must he keep reminding her about the baby? 'I was going by train,' she protested, regretting, even as she heard herself say it, the past tense.

'Don't be silly. You can't possibly carry suitcases. I'll pick you up first thing Friday morning.'

She'd given in to him, as always. Twenty-odd years of being looked after by Robert seemed a hard habit to break. Even now he'd moved in with Gemma who was half his age.

They set off early to avoid the worst of the traffic. Susan knew that, for all his years of driving, Robert was nervous on motorways. She wished he would admit it instead of putting on that guise of bad temper. A little red van shot past them with with never a backward glance, to nick itself neatly into the stream of traffic.

'Stupid bastard,' growled Robert, braking suddenly. Oh God, she thought, it's starting already.

'You feeling alright?'

'Yes, thank you.'

'Got your pills?'

'Yes,' she replied, impatience penetrating her attempts to conceal it. Must he treat her as if she were his aged mother? She'd only had a mild heart attack. It didn't mean she was a total invalid

They hadn't been long on the motorway before the elements began to work against them. The skies closed in, dark and thunderous.

'I think it's going to rain,' Susan intoned, with a wry sideways look at her husband.

'Bloody forecast wrong again.'

Soon it was raining hard, slashing down diagonally. Over to their left, Birmingham was flooded with sunlight where the sky had torn apart. Oncoming headlamps dazzled, and an errant sunbeam catching at the waves from puddles, created tiny, momentary rainbows beside each car. Susan was entranced. She touched his arm, pointing.

'What?' he barked. His hands looked as if they were glued to the steering wheel.

'Nothing,' she sighed.

Then the rainbow came. It was a full one and hung, glowing, against a black curtain of cloud. She recalled the stories her mother used to tell her when she was little. Of the crock of gold at the end of a rainbow, and of children running through its shining arch to happier lands beyond. She remembered her mother's dark brown voice telling her, when times were bad, to 'Think rainbow, darling.' Perhaps this was a good omen. Would things be different in Wales? She wondered how much the others knew. She'd felt unable to confide in anyone. Not even in Jenny, who, of them all, had visited her in the hospital.

'Rob?'

'What?'

'Do Trevor and Cliff know about … about us?' If he'd told his mates, then the girls would know too.'

'No.' The sound came from behind his teeth.

'So, what do you want then? Do we pretend we're still together?'

'We're still married, aren't we?' His tone was one of petulant anger, as if she were winning some argument, and unfairly. Susan was puzzled. She wasn't arguing. 'Anyway, I'm still fond of you, you know that.'

But his voice was not remotely tender. It's just a move in his game, she told herself, and you can be fond of a pet dog. It doesn't mean anything. She turned to look out of the window. It was going to be impossible to fool the girls. They knew her too well.

She must have dozed, for the noisy motorway had gone. They were on a narrow road winding between wooded hills. She could hear water tumbling, and in front of them blue mountains loomed. A strange sense of calm swept over her, almost as if she were coming home. Yet Wales was new to her. It had been Trevor and Mandy's idea to rent a house here for this year's reunion. There would be six, maybe eight, of them this time. They had met up every fifth summer since college. This would be their fourth reunion.

The mountains began to close in, shutting out the green, blocking the sunlight. Isolated sheep stood on the steep, heather-clad slopes, like haricot beans stuck on a collage. Trees gave way to scrub and hawthorn, bowed and beaten. Then came salt and the scent of moon daisies on the air, and at last the sea, glimmering, inviting, impossibly blue.

The house stood alone at the end of a long line of bungalows. It was built of stone with a grey slate roof, and looked as if it had always been there. Moss and lichen covered the garden wall and its many windows were small, like thoughtful eyes.

The front door was flung open and Jenny rushed towards them. She hugged Susan joyfully.

'Isn't it just wonderful here? We're going to have a fabulous time together.' She put one hand up beside her mouth. 'Doug's brought a most peculiar woman. She's called Jo-hanna, and she has mauve hair.' She giggled.

Susan was relieved to find that she and Robert had been allotted single rooms for she would have found sharing intolerable. Descending in the night for a cup of water, she overheard the other girls discussing her.

'Heart trouble's scary.'

'It's largely Robert's fault, anyway.'

'You mean him going off with that young girl?'

'Got her pregnant, didn't he? No problem. Poor Sue.'

'Bastard.'

'How do you know?'

'My daughter, Polly, was at Art school with Gemma when she dropped out.'

'No wonder she looks so down. No kids, no job, no more sports, and no more husband.'

So they had known all the time. Her one consolation was that Robert's subterfuge had been a waste of effort. As the days passed, she grew sensitive to their cosseting, to the hastily concealed concern. When the others went cycling, she strolled over the bridge to Barmouth. When they climbed Cader Idris, she borrowed Mandy's watercolours and sketched the estuary. But it was all, for her, mere displacement. So she didn't have to think about the future. When she did, alone in the narrow bed, it was as dark as the night.

She spent hours trying to capture the fleeting light on the estuary, the criss-crossing currents when the tide flowed in, the changing colours. But all the time, she was aware of sitting on a time bomb, on a spring held tight by her will alone. A mile of ochre sand, hard and wet, gleamed before her, luring her. The strong muscles of her legs ached to stretch and carry her across that golden strand. If only, all those years ago, it had been the gold. To win a silver medal was great, but oh, how she'd wanted the gold.

'I like the way you've made the sandbanks stand out.'

Susan whipped round. She had not heard him approach. He was old, stooped, dressed in black. He had wispy, grey hair and a beard and his skin was yellowish. His eyes were blue and kind and centred on the painting, not her.

'You've a light touch. Have you been painting long?'

'No. But I've always wanted to.' She wondered who he was. Certainly no holiday-maker.

'Rodrig Owen at your service. I have a house here.' He pointed to the stone house. 'But it's let out at the moment.'

'That's where we're staying.'

'So it is.' He was laughing at her.

The next few days it rained, but their last day dawned bright and fair. Susan, unable to sleep, was up and out before six. She trotted along the sea wall towards the promontory. Two herring gulls were squawking over a piece of fish, and down at the water's edge, she glimpsed the crowbacked figure of Rodrig Owen with his little dog. A brisk wind from the west was gathering fresh storm clouds. It would rain again soon and as quickly be fine again. She stooped to pick up a white pebble. It was round and smooth and nestled in her palm like a talisman. So perfect, so beautiful, this place. And she had been so happy here, these past nine days. She didn't want to leave. She could not bear to think of returning to Ilford with its bittersweet memories, to that dismal street of postage-stamp gardens all snipped and hoovered. There was no life for her there, nor anywhere it seemed.

To her right, heavy clouds were drifting in from Ireland. The first specks of rain fell just as the sun rose above the Cader. And there it was again. The rainbow. Scrolling down, soft as chiffon, delicate as watercolour, its seven veils framing a doorway to another world. Clambering down to the hard sand and turning her face to the north, she set her sights on Mawddach Bay, and began to run.

The sheer joy of it. The power flowing through her limbs, its ease and triumph. She was a tiger, a fox before the hounds, she was fleet as a March wind, she was flying. Leaning into the last curve, the roaring of the crowd in her ears and salt in her mouth, she raced towards the finishing line, the sea, and the rainbow.

The pain kicked in suddenly, ravelling down her arm, screwing heart and lungs into a knot of terror. A choking scream and she was down, her cheek on the wet sand. Her whole world was pain. Then, a strange bitterness beneath her tongue, and, very slowly, the vice on her ribcage eased. The warm body of a dog was wedging itself against her and a grey beard brushed her chin. She looked up in time to see the old man replace a silver pillbox in his waistcoat pocket.

'The rainbow...' she began.

'Merely transient phenomena.' He regarded her shrewdly. 'One door only leads to another, you know.'

'I didn't want to leave ...'

'Then don't. Stay on in my house for as long as you need. Be a housekeeper. My room at the pub suits me well enough.'

He helped her to her feet.

'Remember,' he said, as the sun slanted down on them between puffball clouds, 'it's the journey that matters. No more escape routes. You must live your journey to its natural end.' His blue eyes in their dark pouches shone. 'And be joyful.'

*Mary Rothwell*

# Gabriel

Each time Peter walks up the short drive to the door of his former home the ghosts of his past walk alongside him. Wraiths and changing phantoms of what might have been, they lurk in brickwork, in the unkempt garden, in the emptied wardrobe and drawers of the room at the top of the stairs. They linger beside gooseberry bushes and the yellow standard rose which he planted on Miriam's thirtieth birthday. They linger in the path down the back garden where he and Ben wrote "Ben, Miriam, Peter" in broken china.

He puts his key in the lock, waits for it to turn, for the door to open. It resists. He checks the key and tries again. And again. Stupid bloody woman, she's changed the lock. What's possessed her? He kicks the door and winces as pain shoots through his foot. How bloody dare she? Doesn't she realise he only comes round because he's concerned about her, because he cares for her? And two books that are vital for tomorrow's lecture are upstairs in his study.

Another layer of skin is peeling off his nose. He should have told Miriam he was going to Tenerife. One more item to add to the list of things he hasn't plucked up courage to tell her. Like why he left her four months previously. He tried to but she wasn't listening. How do you tell the woman you have been married to for thirteen years that she is drowning you in her sea of grief? That, even now, in a different bed, you waken from a recurring nightmare in which she is dragging you under with her.

He hops from one foot to another. Twenty past four. Where the hell is she? She always comes home straight from school. Doesn't like driving in the dark. The back door's locked too, bolted on the inside. She's become neurotic about burglars since he left, but she hasn't been careful enough. The small kitchen window's not properly latched. He picks up a chisel from his tools in the outhouse, stands on a bucket and releases the catch. Then it's simply a matter of reaching down and opening the lower part of the window.

He prepares to climb in, head first. Shoulders through. Easy, does it.

Shit, his bum's jammed. He twists. He turns and panics. What if Miriam finds him, the broad seat of his jeans framed like a dirty postcard in the window? With a thigh-skinning wrench he frees himself. His hands flay over the draining board. A bowl smashes in jagged pieces on the floor where something moves.

A scaly neck, topped by a bald head. Gabriel, fixing him with that basilisk stare of his! Why the hell is Gabriel inside?

'Don't look at me like that, you ugly brute.' He throws a fork at the creature. Gabriel retracts his head and plays dead, the patterned shell expressionless as a dinner plate. A flush of shame washes over Peter.

*'How long do tortoises live, Daddy?' Ben asked.*

*'Some tortoises in Africa live much longer than human beings. Some species live for centuries.'*

*'Will Gabriel live for hundreds of years, Daddy? Longer than me?'*

*He took Ben to the library and showed him pictures of various types of tortoise, some measuring only eight or ten inches like Gabriel, some big enough for a man to sit on. They made a scrapbook of different types of turtles and tortoises and Miriam pasted "Gabriel's Family" on the cover.*

*After the accident the scrapbook and all Ben's toys and clothes, all his possessions, were given to the NSPCC.*

*'No shrines, Miriam. Remember, we agreed. We have to get on with our lives.' He gently put his arms round her rigid shoulders as the van prepared to move away, but he couldn't stop her snatching back the cardboard box, the one covered with pictures Ben had painted of Gabriel.*

*'Gabriel's not a possession. He's alive. He belongs here same as Ben did.' She cradled the box the way she used to cradle Ben.*

Upstairs, Peter goes into his study. From the top shelf he takes "Linguistics in Context" and "Linguistics and English Grammar." The room is as he left it. Pencils sharpened, pens in holders. He could reach out in pitch darkness and put his hand on sellotape, stapler, discs, paper clips. His blind fingers could select a precise reference book from the shelves. It's his study, his sanctuary, yet he's uneasy, not quite belonging, not quite an intruder in what fees like alien territory.

He scans the empty street again and the old feeling of impatience flares in him. What's she's playing at? It will be dark soon. There's no beer in the fridge, not that Miriam drinks beer but she always has some for him. He pours a tumbler of sweet sherry and grimaces. Each mouthful thickens his

- 20 -

tongue. The aftertaste cloys. He eases buttock-clenching jeans down over his knees and gasps with relief. Blood blisters glisten over his raw-red thighs. They hurt like hell and his toe aches. Sally, the woman he had hoped would accompany him to Tenerife, said jeans took years off him. He squirms in the armchair, which over the years has moulded itself to his shape. Miriam's absence oppresses him. Without her fussing around with offers of tea, cake, sandwiches, or a cooked meal, without her sad, soft voice, the house is lifeless, an empty building whose beating pulse has stopped. What's the matter with him? He misses her. He even misses her martyred silences, her litany of disasters: 'The kitchen tap's dripping.' 'The telly's on the blink again.' 'The garage door's coming off its hinges.'

Gabriel's stare unnerves him. It reminds him of the unspoken accusations in Miriam's eyes that helped to drive him away. She knows perfectly well that Gabriel shouldn't be inside. He explained very clearly to her and to Ben why tortoises need to hibernate in winter.

He lurches at the animal. Its head disappears inside the shell.

'Think you're a bleeding ostrich? Well, I'll show you.'

Shuddering at the thought of the soft body inside, he grabs the shell, holds it at arm's length and stomps outside. The creature's elephantine legs paw the air; they writhe all the way to the bottom of the garden. When he drops it over the fence into the field, its chill flesh grazes his hand.

Back at college, the common room and his colleagues' rooms are empty. In the pub he stands among strangers, whose rowdy jollity infects the space around him. Some glance at watches, say it's time to go home and they leave with 'See you tomorrow.' 'Take care, mate.'

The beer he orders turns to vinegar in his mouth. Gabriel might die, suddenly plunged without warning into the chill night and Miriam will be terrified to find the back door unlocked and Gabriel gone. He's a shit, a vindictive, self-centred, callous shit. Poor girl, she's had more than enough to enough to cope with. Leaving barely tasted beer on the counter he hurries to the house, parks the car at the roadside and rushes round the back. A light flashes on. He stops dead, legs splayed, arms rigid, an escaping prisoner trapped in a searchlight's beam. What's the matter with him? He knows how a sensor works. Poor Miriam, for years she wanted him to fit one. He'd meant to, but he'd been too bone-idle. Too busy doing what he thought was important.

Out of the glare of the light, he stumbles down the path towards the field where he deposited Gabriel. He has forgotten the overgrown gooseberry bush that almost straddles the path. He has forgotten how sharp its thorns are.

'Gabriel, Gabriel!' He paces back and forth the length of the fence, calling into the night. On his knees he gropes though dank grass. 'Gabriel, come back. Please. There's a good chap. Please come back. Please.' He listens, peers unseeing through silent darkness.

Nothing stirs. He shuffles towards the house and stops in his tracks as the light flashes on again. He moves out of its range and crouches against the outhouse, still pleading with Gabriel to come back

A car speeds into the street, engine roaring. Its tyres squeal. It skids outside his home and ice penetrates his skin. He waits for the clash of metal against metal. For the sound of screams.

*It had been his fault. From across the road, he saw Ben running down the drive to meet him. He heard him call, 'Daddy, Daddy'.*

*He saw the moving car. He saw his son rush from behind a parked van into its path.*

*'Go back, Ben! Go back!' Every sinew of his body yelled, but no sound came. No sound came.*

The car revs down the street. Soon it's out of earshot, but he can't stop shivering. His whole body has turned to ice. Miriam's a nervous driver. What if some other maniac crashes into her and his entire family is wiped out. First Ben, then Gabriel…

An hour passes. White light drenches the back of the house. From the shadows he stares into the dazzling semi-circle. No one. Nothing. The sensor must be faulty. He'll have to fix it. Miriam will be terrified if the bloody thing comes on of its own accord during the night. Suddenly he's aware of a movement at the edge of the glare, a movement so imperceptible he almost missed it in his panic, and his heart leaps for joy. One foreleg barely passing the other, neck at full stretch as if drawn by a magnet, Gabriel is inching his way over the patio, steering an unerring course towards the back door.

*In the last page of Ben's scrapbook was an entry copied from the Encyclopaedia Britannica in his rounded handwriting:*
*'The tortoise has good sight. It easily distinguishes between differences and intensity of light. Most species have a "home area" to which they return if taken a short distance away.'*

'Gabriel, you little beauty. You've come back.' Peter bends down, picks up the tortoise and hugs him against his chest, stroking his unyielding carapace. He carries him into the kitchen and lays him in his box. His hand hovers above him, loath to lose contact. Gabriel withdraws and settles into his bed. Peter glances at his watch. Only ten past eight. He goes to his car to wait for Miriam away from the light of the street lamp.

At half past nine, she turns into the drive and gets out. She's alone, thank God!

Miriam,' he calls. 'Miriam,' he repeats, not knowing what else to say, not daring to cross the line which separates the footpath from the drive.

She starts and her hand, about to lock the car, falls to her side. She calls his name and takes several tentative steps towards him.

'Peter, what's the matter? What's wrong?' She squints, as though unable to focus on his face. 'Peter, you're crying? What's happened? Don't cry. Please don't cry.'

Like pent-up water through an opened flood-gate, his tears fall. He weeps for his ten-year-old son who came second in the egg and spoon race at his school's Sports Day, whose Rs sounded like Ls when he spoke quickly, whose knees were always crusted with scabs. He weeps for his once laughing wife, for the songs she no longer sings, for the other children she might have had. And he weeps for himself. For his blindness, his stupidity and for the pain he has caused.

'Don't cry, Peter. I can't bear to see you cry. Everything will be all right. You'll see.'

Miriam takes his hand. She puts her key into the lock and guides him into the hall as she would a frightened child. The door closes quietly behind them.

*Monica Percy*

# Reflections

Sophie surveyed herself critically in the mirror. Calm grey eyes stared back. Calm! How could they be calm? It must show. Surely, it must. Some sign, some indication? No. Her hair needed washing, she'd meant to do that yesterday, but there hadn't been the time. There was never the time. That obstinate tuft at the side of her head still refusing to lie flat, refusing to stay still, just as normal. She patted it absentmindedly.

Perhaps she was slightly paler than usual? She looked closer. No, no paler. Sallow, yes. No bright, rosy, apple cheeks for her. No, she'd never had those. Not like Amy Patterson. Amy Patterson! Oh goodness, what a time to think about Amy. How could she have forgotten Amy, they were inseparable at junior school? Those long, thick ringlets of hers, always tied with bright shiny ribbons. Yes, every night when Amy went to bed her mother tied her hair in tissue paper, and every morning twisted the ringlets and put on fresh ribbons.

Sophie looked at her reflection. How she'd prayed every night for ringlets like Amy's. It never did any good, when she woke up the wispy haystack was still there. Oh my, and how she'd also wished she had a mother like Amy's. Her mother never had the patience to do ringlets for her. Well, come to that, there'd never been any tissue paper in the house, let alone going to bed covered in it. Sophie looked at herself again. Hair grey now, but at least the perm gave it a bit more body.

She wondered what had happened to Amy? Marjory Evans said she went off in an old van to Spain with an artist, but she'd never believed it, not of Amy. Her mother wouldn't have liked that. No. And her dad would never have stood for it. Amy's mum and dad … they were nice, always pleased to see her. Not like her own mum and dad. Always shouting, and swearing, at each other, never happy like Amy's mum and dad. They were always happy. Always happy… Hmm. Amy Patterson. A bright shiny girl with bright shiny ribbons.

'You've never been shiny,' she said to herself. 'You might be Sophie

Simpson now, not Sophie Brown, but you're still brown, still dull, always were, always will be.' She peered in the mirror again. Where had that child gone, the one who loved Amy Patterson? When had her skin turned so sallow? She couldn't remember. It had happened gradually, imperceptibly, like everything else. Like the lines that etched their way across her face. Showing character they say. Showing the trample of time more like. Time marching on, relentlessly! No turning back.

No, you can't turn back now. Bridges burnt. You've made your bed, now you must lie in it. That was Mother's favourite saying. 'No point in complaining,' she'd say, 'You've made your bed, Miss, now you must lie in it'. She could never do anything right for her, she was always nagging, always criticising. 'Can't you do something with that hair, girl, you're not going out like that.' On and on she went. Didn't even stop after she got married.

Sophie sighed and looked in the mirror again. What about the lips, did they show anything? They were Mother's lips. Thin, and pressed tightly together, with small lines radiating out to meet others. She forced a smile, and for an instant the whole image changed. Except the eyes, except the truth, except reality. The smile drained from her face.

She went to the drinks cabinet, quietly, carefully, every movement magnified, slow and laborious. Opening the door she took out a bottle. 'I shouldn't be drinking at this time of day,' she thought briefly, looking towards the kitchen. Her hand hesitated over the glass for a second. 'Why not,' she said to herself, as she grasped the glass firmly and quietly poured herself a large sherry.

Crossing to the chair, she sat down. Closing her eyes she took a sip of the pale liquid. With every mouthful the burden eased, lifted, floated away. She giggled to herself as she opened her eyes. The room looked just the same, clean, tidy, just like a new pin. That's how John liked it. Everything in its place and a place for everything. Ship-shape. She giggled again. She knew where her place was too. A woman's place is in the home! The home! A woman's place is in the house. Housewife. Housework. Cleaning, polishing, cooking, washing. Always busy, always on the go. Busy bee. Busy bee.

She could see John through the open kitchen door. Corduroy trousers, check shirt she'd ironed last Thursday. Brown shoes. She'd always liked those shoes. Where did they buy them? Oh yes, that smart new shop in town. They'd seen them in the window. John liked the look of them and marched straight in, her trailing behind. She always trailed behind. It was a very expensive shop. Very expensive shoes too. 'They'll last a long time,' John said. Yes, they'll last a long time. She took another mouthful of sherry.

John always led the way. That's what she'd liked about him when they first met. He knew so much about everything. He was clever, not like her. She didn't know anything very much. That's why she'd been overwhelmed when he asked her to marry him. 'Fancy someone like John wanting to marry me,' she'd thought when he'd asked her. She couldn't remember saying yes, she didn't have to. John knew what she wanted. He'd worked it all out, got it all planned: where they would live, what furniture they would have. He was very good at that sort of thing, knew just what went with what. Lovely. It would have been nice if they'd had a few roses in the garden though. Yes, she would have liked that. John said they were too much trouble. All that pruning. Best to have evergreens, much better, something to look at all year. He was right of course, but roses were very pretty.

How happy she'd been in the beginning. She'd given up her job straight away. John didn't want a wife of his to work. 'Well, what would they think in the bank?' he'd said, and of course he was right. She was pleased to give it up, after all it wasn't a proper job. Not like his, and of course, when they had a family, well, a mother shouldn't work. Only they'd never had a family. The time had never been right. Then somehow it was too late. At first John had liked talking to her about things, telling her what was what. It was only later that her stupidity got on his nerves; she knew how much she irritated him. Well she had nothing interesting to say had she, stuck at home all day.

She lifted the glass to her mouth again and another giggle bubbled up. 'Be quiet. Yes, I must keep quiet, John doesn't like noise,' she said to herself. 'Don't keep banging about, do that quietly, I can't hear the telly.' How many times had John said that? Too many times to count. 'Be seen and not heard.' She heard her father's voice. She'd always had to be seen and not heard. 'You're no good.' 'You're not wanted.' 'I don't want you.' The words rang in her ears. The giggle turned into a sob. Trembling, she lifted the glass and drained the contents.

What's the time? She looked at the clock. Only half past eleven? Surely it must be later than that. She looked down at her watch. Eleven thirty! She got up from the chair, crossed the room to the window, and looked out. There was the front garden, the hedge hiding the busy road where cars and life rushed by. Everything as usual. An ordinary day. The sun is shining. It shouldn't be shining. It should be cloudy. Wasn't it cloudy when she'd got up? She couldn't remember. It seemed so long ago: a lifetime ago!

She smiled to herself. Yes. John had complained about the weather when he got up. No, 'Good morning, dear,' from him. His first words were complaints about the weather, as if it was her fault. The weather, the toast,

- 26 -

everything. 'You're to blame.' 'It's all your fault.' Things were always her fault. Always had been!

Sophie moved away from the window, went to the mirror and looked at her reflection again. She was suddenly aware of her hands, clenched tightly by her sides, knuckles white, arms stiff. Breathing in deeply she tried to relax her shoulders. Any other sign of tension? Neck? Shoulders? No, not now, the unremarkable, familiar, slightly overweight reflection gazed back. Surely there must be some sign, something different? Perhaps a slight tremble, hardly perceptible? No, that had stopped now. Just calm, just ordinary, just her, except it wasn't ordinary, not anymore.

Sophie looked towards the kitchen again. Yes, John was still there. She looked away. Well, what now? She looked slowly round the room. Window, fireplace, coffee table, door, telephone. Telephone! Yes that's it. She went over, picked up the telephone book and flicked through the pages. Yes there it was. She slowly lifted the receiver and pressed the buttons. Ringing tone. Click. 'Walton Police Station.'

She took a deep breath. 'Hallo, this is Mrs Simpson, Brook Cottage. I think I've killed my husband.'

*Janet Tredinnick*

# The Home Décor Wars

He wanted simplicity
Bare brick, spare fittings
clinical interiors
The minimalist thing
Sunlight and mirrors
She had other ideas

Plush, pile-carpets
Mats, hats, castanets
Some maracas from Caracas
A collection of Russian dolls
enlarging, expanding
coveting unconquered space
with glassy Slavic eyes

He watched the advance
of ornaments and oddments
fretful, resentful
his hopes of open space
and natural light
fading fast

'How about a Spring clean?'
he suggested, uselessly

Her weekend trip, the hired skip
It had seemed a good idea
at the time.

First, just words were thrown
then a Russian doll
rare escapee of his cull
strafed his face
Further items followed.

Now peering, pining
from his exiled space
the place they'd shared
distantly visible
he wanted to return
to restate the case
for mirrors and sunlight
he wanted to
excavate, extricate her
from the mounting
nonsense, he imagined
expanded, extended
barring all exits.

*John Enefer*

# Icarus Heart

I turned,
Silver blind from winter sun,
Ice cold on millpond sea,
And I saw your heart
Had taken flight on Icarus wings,
Safe in that chill sky.
I was the one who fell.

*Richard Wheeler*

# The Right Ear of Malchus

My grandfather always seemed an old man. I remember him sitting outside the house beside the door. Whatever the weather he had a cloth about his head. It kept the wind and sand from him in the cool weather and the heat of the sun from him when it was hot. His face was weather-beaten from so much time spent outside. It hadn't always been like that. Much of his working life was spent inside the Temple serving the High Priest, helping him with the rituals of the Temple, to prepare sacrifices, to oversee necessities for the scattering of blood and water, the cleansing and the purifying, what Grandfather called 'the making of all things right.'

My father should have worked in the Temple too, learning from his father, following in his father's footsteps. But there was such a happening in the city, such a blast of words and hatred, such a scattering of all the routine and ritual, it was impossible for my father to be accepted.

I've heard my mother say that when it all happened the rage against my grandfather was so terrible the family had to hide in the hills. For a time they lived like beggars on wild fruit and berries and what little they could prevail on passing travellers to spare. And none of it was Grandfather's fault.

As time passed and the rumours died down he was able sit in peace outside his own dwelling once again. Always he had his staff between his knees, his hands crossed over the top of it, always the left hand over the right one. When he was tired he would lean forward, his chin resting on his hands. Sometimes the small leather pouch he wore perpetually round his neck would swing forward. He would sit upright again so that it fell back into the folds of his robe. He liked it kept close to his heart like a secret.

His eyes were failing, but still they stared into the distance as though watching for the return of a loved one. He would have stayed there watching day and night, but my mother made him eat and sleep. She used to take him by the arm and gently coax him into the house. Then she would lead him to the table of food set out for the men and encourage him to eat. Later she would guide him to his bed.

When I came of age I had to help my mother prepare the food. I would rather have been out walking in the hills or sitting beside my grandfather listening to his stories of the past. But my mother told me I must learn how to do all the womanly things, tasks I would perform one day in my own home for a husband and family.

As I grew from a baby I became my grandfather's favourite. No one told me so. It was just something I always knew. I'm the quiet one, the only girl. My brothers are noisy, always chattering. They go out into the fields and work with my father, heavy back-breaking work in our poor soil, growing beans and leeks, onions and garlic. Sometimes the older ones are allowed to go to the big city, a long walk by dusty road, to sell the surplus produce in the market. They set out early in the morning, the ass laden with vegetables. Despite the early start it still means a night spent away from home with Uncle Bartimaeus, our father's youngest brother who lives in the city. The boys come back full of gossip gathered from the market and news of kinsmen. And they bring fruit, figs and dates and pomegranates, the things we cannot grow.

Because I'm a girl I'm not expected to join in the talking, but must sit quietly in the corner. I help my mother to spin the wool from the sheep, or else I sit beside her, watching and learning, as she weaves ancient family patterns on her loom. Like the patterns, the loom has been handed down from mother to daughter through the years. One day it will be mine and I shall make the cloth. I wish Grandfather were still here to see me growing up.

He would ignore me when the men came home in the evening, but during the day when they were away at work in the fields I would have my quiet times with him. Sometimes he would just sit. Sometimes friends would call. After greetings had been exchanged and food and drink offered, Grandfather would ask me to bring out his games board so they could play a game together. I would put the board on its stand to the left of grandfather's chair and set out the counters the way he taught me. I still don't understand the rules of the games, but I love to study the board with its beautiful patterns made of shells. I was happy when Grandfather won. He used to smile and pat my head as though I had helped him.

When the board had been put away and the talking had finished I would stay close by his side, patiently waiting for one of his stories. He seldom disappointed me. Sometimes he told about an encounter with a wild boar while he travelled to deliver an important paper for the High Priest; or about how he first came to the Temple as a small boy. Sometimes it would be a story about the High Priest losing important keys, and how at the last minute before they were needed Grandfather would find them. His favourite story, which he told again and again although it caused all the turmoil, was the story of his right ear. This was a tale just for me. I never heard him share it with anyone else.

It was about an evening long ago when he was still the High Priest's servant. The High Priest had been asked to arrange for the arrest of a fanatic who had been stirring up trouble in the district for weeks. Grandfather, still a young man at this time, was directed to arm himself and accompany a band of men appointed to carry out the arrest. Despite having a stave at the ready, and knowing the men around him had swords and staves, my grandfather was terrified. He told me his hands shook so much he could hardly light his lantern. He was a strong young man and no coward, but the talk in the Temple of the man's startling behaviour had frightened everyone. They went out of the city and into a wild and distant garden where few people ventured after dark.

Grandfather was surprised when they came on the wanted man. He couldn't believe they had found the right one. 'I wish you could have seen him, Marisa,' he would say to me. 'He was fresh-faced, softly spoken, polite to all those round him. He didn't attempt to escape or to fight his captors, although some of his followers had swords. He could have slipped away into the darkness and left them to fight for him.'

Grandfather had hung back, expecting to find a savage, but when he saw this gentle, kindly man he felt compelled towards him. 'I couldn't help myself,' he would tell me. 'It was almost as though I was being pushed. I wanted to kneel and touch the man's feet, so I stepped towards him.'

The next moment was terrible. Perhaps his move had been misunderstood. Perhaps they thought he intended to strike the criminal. One of the wanted man's followers raised his sword and cut through the air with it. The sword caught my grandfather's ear and sliced it off so that it fell to the ground.

When grandfather told this part of the story his face would darken and his eyes almost close as he relived the pain of that blow. 'I stumbled and almost fell,' he would say. 'I put my hand up and felt the warm blood trickling down my neck.' At this point he would tremble and have to close his eyes and remain quiet for minutes before he could continue. I used to lean against him and put my hand on his to comfort him.

When he had recovered he would carry on with his story and tell me how the fanatic was seized and held by the priests' men without a struggle. But then he shouted, 'No more of this!' Grandfather said it was the only time he heard him raise his voice. The men from the Temple were beginning to tie him up, but he quietly asked to be released. His voice and manner were so compelling their leader nodded his head and the men let go of him.

What happened next was like a miracle. This gentle man reached down and picked up the ear and put it back into place on Grandfather's head. 'For a moment he held it there, Marisa,' Grandfather would say. 'And when that man looked straight into my eyes with a radiant expression on his face, all the pain and blood vanished as if the wound had never been.'

I loved this part of the story and I always hoped Grandfather would follow it with a happy ending, but he never did. He said they took the criminal away and he had a cruel and lingering death. That used to make Grandfather sad and his eyes would fill with tears as he said it. I felt sad, too, because I couldn't believe he was a wicked man or he wouldn't have done such a kind and marvellous thing for my grandfather.

Once, when I pretended to doubt the story just to tease Grandfather, he unwound his head cloth and pulled his wispy grey hair aside to show the thin white scar that ran all round the ear, so fine and neat one had to look closely to see it.

I believe the story because my grandfather told it and I know he was a truthful man, but I still puzzle about how it was done. I asked Grandfather many times, but he couldn't tell me. Now he's dead and I shall never know the answer. But he told me one last story before he died.

At the end of the dry season, when the weather was threatening to break, everyone else was out in the fields working to get the last of the crops in before the rain came. I had been left to care for Grandfather. He was restless and seemed very tired, but unable to sleep. I asked for a story thinking it would pass the time for him, but he shook his head. I hoped someone would come by and I could get the games board and counters out, but everyone young enough to work was in the fields and the air was too hot and dry for old people to be walking about.

I sat with him outside the house, one hand on his two dry and withered ones, one hand fanning his face with a leaf to cool him. Eventually he did sleep, and still I fanned him. The sleep was shallow and he appeared to be dreaming. Then he called out a name I didn't recognise and can't now remember. Suddenly he was awake and seemed refreshed.

'Perhaps it is time for one last story,' he said to me with a smile. 'Remember your favourite, the one about my ear?' I nodded and he smiled again. 'This is not really a new story,' he said. 'Just more of that old one.'

And he began. 'I was amazed when my ear was restored. I wanted to tell everyone. It seemed like a miracle to me. I went back to the Temple full of excitement, longing to tell the priests what had happened. But I was shut out. The High Priest sent a servant to tell me I was no longer fit to work there. I asked to see the High Priest for myself, but was told to go away. I couldn't understand what was happening, but at first I was too excited to be troubled. I went on telling everyone I met what had happened to me, but they all turned away. They seemed too frightened to listen.' Here Grandfather paused and asked for a drink. He sipped from the beaker of milk I brought him from our goat and seemed lost in thought.

'It was all so long ago,' he said, 'And perhaps best forgotten.'

He pulled the leather pouch from his robe and studied it while I pleaded with him to carry on. 'Well, just for you, Marisa,' he said. 'Now your grandmother is buried no one else knows exactly what happened.

'That night I wrapped myself in my cloak and slept in the street outside the Temple. The next morning, certain that my rejection the day before had been a mistake, I tried again to get in, but my way was barred. Then a messenger from the High Priest came to me. He told me I could return to my work so long as I stopped telling lies about what had happened in the garden the night before. If anyone asked me I must deny my ear had ever been cut off - or restored.

'I couldn't understand why I should do that. I thought a long time about it. Losing my job would be a disgrace to the family and mean poverty for us all. I had already begun to prepare my eldest son, your father, to take part in the Temple rituals. It would be a loss to him, too.'

All day Grandfather wandered about on the outskirts of the city, keeping well away from the crowds that had gathered for the Feast of Unleavened Bread. But he knew it was no good putting things off. In the early evening he returned to the Temple and told the priests that he couldn't do what they had asked of him. 'All my life, Marisa, I have sought to tell the truth. I told them I couldn't do anything else.'

"Then you must go back to your family," they told me. "We have no place for you here." So I began to walk back to my wife and children who lived outside the city.

'Soon it was dark. I had a lantern, but the road was rough. I stumbled and dropped my lantern, so it went out. While I was feeling about in the dark to recover it I was set on by a band of ruffians. They held me fast and put my right hand on a rock. My middle finger was chopped off with a blow from a large knife. "You say your king replaced your ear for you," they said.

- 35 -

"See if he can put your finger back on." I fainted with the pain and when I recovered my senses the men had gone. I staggered home and fell into the house.

'Your grandmother bathed my wound and wrapped my hand in cloths with an ointment of myrrh until the stump had healed. Perhaps I was a foolish man, but I believed it was possible to have my finger restored to my hand as my ear had been. I was ill with a fever for some days, but as I drifted in and out of consciousness I persuaded your grandmother to part with some of our meagre savings. She had my finger embalmed against the time when I could seek out the healer of my ear.

'As soon as I was well enough I went back to the city and made enquiries for him. With great sadness I learnt that he had been crucified, a particularly horrible form of death handed out by Roman law. His followers had all gone into hiding and I was shunned by everyone I asked for information. After my fruitless search I returned home to find the family sheltering in a cave, having been hounded out of our home by vagabonds in the employment of the Temple. I had had my suspicions earlier. I only had a brief glimpse of the knife used to remove my finger, but it was enough for me to recognise it as one of the special instruments kept in the Temple for the sacrificial killing of animals.

'We fled to the hills and lived like outlaws for three years until your Uncle Bartimaeus, a young man then, sent to say he judged it was safe for us to return. Our house had been destroyed, but we carted what was left of the stones to this lonely spot. We lived in the cave that had sheltered the family earlier until we had built a house fit for my son's bride. It was the house where later you were born, Marisa.

'Now I am an old man and near to death. I still keep my finger in this leather pouch about my neck. I clung on to hope because there was talk about that wonderful man returning to life. I don't know whether he was man or god or king. But after our brief meeting I believed he was capable of anything. And didn't he prove it to me by restoring my ear?'

*Gwenda J Lee*

# The Mission

### Introduction
*There are many stories in which troops have been dropped behind enemy lines. This is an account of one such event, arguably the best known of them all. Although clearly the narrator is fictitious, all the other characters and incidents described have been recorded in many documents. For obvious reasons the names of the characters involved have been omitted.*

We sat on the hard wooden benches in two rows opposite one another. Twelve men either side and the commander at the end facing down the narrow corridor between us. After nearly fifteen hours cramped in that tiny space, the smell of humanity was nauseous. But the smell of fear was stronger.

After so many years of war, this mission was a last attempt to break the stalemate and deal a final blow to the enemy. Each one of us was aware of the importance of success. We also knew that if things went wrong, the only alternative was death.

We had been hand-picked for the job. Drawn from different allied commands, each one of us was battle-hardened and had led many assaults on the enemy lines over the previous years. Now we sat together in these cramped conditions, our helmets on our laps and our weapons clasped between our knees, wondering what this night would bring.

It was barely possible to sit upright. The walls of the transporter curved behind our backs and over our heads, to form what felt like a long, gloomy, cylindrical tomb. The only space was in one of the side walls, where a tightly sealed door reminded us of the hazardous drop we would shortly have to make.

When we had climbed into our positions, just before dawn, there had been a tense feeling of suspense, which we could relieve by banter between ourselves in the time honoured fashion. As we had been towed to our destination the noise outside had kept our senses alert. Twice there had been loud bangs, too close for comfort. Earlier an enemy missile had penetrated the curved walls of our tomb, narrowly missing the man next to me.

Now the towing had finished and we were silently poised in the air waiting for the signal to disembark. It was the enforced silence that played on our tautly stretched nerves, producing that bitter-sweet taste of fear. In the silence of the night, one sound could give warning of our approach to the enemy and all would be lost.

In an attempt to distract my mind from thinking of the dangers to come, I thought about my companions. All of them had won battle honours and most of them had wives and children at home praying for their safe return. In the darkness I couldn't see them, but I could sense the men close to me.

The man to my left had shown no outward sign of fear even when his earlier brush with death had occurred. His father, whose bravery was legendary, had been killed earlier in the war. The son was clearly cast in the same mould.

At the other end of the scale, the man opposite me was trembling with terror. Before the war he had been a skilled craftsman and an amateur boxer of considerable fame. Despite his prowess with his fists, the man was a braggart and a coward. He alone had been forced to come on this mission, as the commander needed his skills for the task we were about to undertake. At the last moment it had been necessary to force him aboard, under the threat of execution for desertion.

The commander was not the highest ranking officer on the mission. The man sitting to his left was superior in rank, but clearly not in ability. He had begged to come, fully accepting the commander's authority. But then, he had a personal stake in the whole affair. No-one challenged the commander's authority. His leadership throughout the war had been an inspiration to us all. But his success was due to cunning as much as bravery. I could sense those shrewd eyes, somehow piercing the gloom, as they assessed the situation and watched for any sign of trouble. It was he who had thought out the plan for this mission. He had arranged to plant an agent behind the enemy lines who was to make contact with a disillusioned commander from their ranks. Our safety depended on these two men, a spy and a traitor. At least so far they had not let us down.

A mute signal from the commander must have been passed along the rank of men opposite. The terrified man facing me silently moved to the hatch door and, after nervously fiddling with the fastenings, opened it. The cool night air blew onto our faces, giving welcome relief from the claustrophobic feelings we had been experiencing. There was also a tangible relief of tension as we realised the action was about to begin.

What happened next took us all by surprise. The youngest member of our party moved towards the open door, stumbled, and fell through it head first. Another man had been about to shout a warning, but the commander had clapped a great hand over his mouth to silence him. The youth had not uttered a sound as he plunged to certain death, and we waited tensely, to see if the enemy had spotted his fall.

The moment passed, and our training took over as we all acted to the pre-arranged plan. In turn we each moved to that open hatch, paused for three seconds, and then plunged into the inky blackness below.

On the ground, we thanked the Gods that we had arrived without detection. Then, hastily pulling on our battle gear, we dispersed through the silent streets of Troy.

*Michael Smith*

### Characters and Incidents

*The characters and incidents in this story are, as stated in the introduction, based on many historical documents including: Homer, Livy, Virgil, Ovid, Euripides and Plutarch.*

# Poppies

'Thank God for his letters.' Emma turned to her dearest friend sitting on the grass beside her. 'At least I know he's safe. It's been four months now and only three letters.' She waved the latest piece of blue paper in the air. 'Why just three letters? And why only one page in each? He tells me nothing Rose, nothing.' Tears filled her eyes.

'Now come on Emma,' Rose put her arm round Emma's shoulders. 'Who knows the reason? Maybe they're told only to write short letters, maybe –'

'But he doesn't say anything Rose, I don't know what he's doing, don't know if he's getting enough to eat, going to the front line, or actually fighting. Oh God, what if … ?'

'Probably he's not allowed, have you thought of that? Maybe all the letters are vetted, or whatever they call it.'

'Yes, but it's wrong, we should know what's happening - it isn't fair.'

'But you do know what he's doing for heaven's sake, look, look here.' She grabbed the letter from Emma. 'He says he's sitting in his bunker, drinking a mug of tea while he's writing to you. And down here,' she pointed further down the page, 'see, he says he's helping his captain make a garden.'

'Yes, but -'

'Making a garden in the middle of a war. Imagine!' She smiled. 'What a good idea, it'll cheer everybody up. That captain's got a lot of sense. Mind you, officers are supposed to do things like that, I mean, you know, keep things as normal as possible.'

Emma looked up. 'Yes, and Willie will love it, he's always pottering around in the garden.' Then she frowned. 'But it's not really a garden is it? They're only transplanting some flowers from the gardens of the big house they've been staying in.'

'But they're going to take them to the headquarters near the reserve trenches, aren't they? It's bound to bring a little bit of home, make things seem more normal, and if they're doing that, they're not fighting. So come on, cheer up, stop being so gloomy.'

'Yes, I suppose,' Emma said. 'Probably.' She looked at Rose. 'I wonder what flowers they have over there?'

'Just the same as here, silly.' Rose rolled her eyes. 'It's only over the water in Belgium. It's the best time of year for flowers, so there's lots around: pansies, petunias, marigolds, sunflowers.'

'Yes, maybe even lavender,' added Emma wistfully. She shivered and pulled her shawl around her. 'It's getting cold, Rose, will we go back?'

'Mmm, you're right, the wind's getting up. Let's go then.' They lifted themselves up from the grass and turned towards the village.

'Oh it's beautiful isn't it, Emma?' Rose pointed down over the myriad greens of the fields, the moorland, with its misty hues of creamy coloured broom and purple heathers, to the village beneath the hills.

'Yes, it is, so peaceful - but oh, Rose, Willie must miss it terribly - and –' She stopped, feeling the tears come again.

'I know, but he'll be home soon.' Rose caught hold of Emma's hand. 'Come on, cheer up, they say it'll be over by Christmas.'

'Yes, but they said that last year, when it all started, remember? Oh, it's awful, you don't know what to believe.'

'Well, I believe it will, and just think, what a surprise he'll have!' Playfully she patted Emma's tummy, then suddenly she grabbed her arm.

'Oh, look, look over there.' Rose was pointing over the wide expanse of fern and bracken to a cornfield, where long-stemmed scarlet flowers waved gently.

'Yes, I remember seeing a few around the outskirts of the field last year Rose, but now there are hundreds. What are they called again?'

'I'm not sure, but I saw masses of them last year in Kinross; remember, when Eddie and me went to see his auntie?'

Emma nodded. 'Yes, I remember.'

'Well, I think they're the same, I remember the colour, so bright. Let's go and see if we can pick some.' She hurried towards the field.

The clouds were rolling in the sky, dark and warm, threatening rain.

'Just look at their colour,' Emma shouted as she reached the field, the red glare of the flowers stabbing her eyes.

The wind moaned and made her shiver: So red, like blood. She stopped and touched. So soft. 'What are they called?' she whispered.

'Poppies,' the young captain says to me. 'I'm taking some seeds, see if they'll grow in pots, maybe take some home when this bloody war ends. Gorgeous colour, really bright, eh?'

'They are that, sir, lovely and bright, dazzlin' almost,' and I carry on packin' the pots with geraniums and nasturtiums. Easy number this, fetchin' and carryin', wish I was home though, in ma own garden. Wonder what Em's up to? Probably the washin', or maybe bakin' soda scones; could just do with a couple, thick with butter. She could be in the garden, could be doin' just what I'm doin' - hope so, doesn't make her feel so far away.

I watch the captain potterin' around in the garden of the fine house we call *The Chateau*, on the western outskirts of Ypres where the officers of the second Camerons are billeted, while the battalion is at rest. Tomorrow it'll be back to the trenches. Wonder what he feels about that? Can't say, he always looks the same, always cheerful, hardly ever shouts. Nice chap for an officer. I'm scared half to death. Wonder if he's scared? Still, wouldn't tell me if he was. Daren't.

It's pretty good here. I stretch and look around. The garden's hardly damaged and the place is ablaze with flowers. There's even some delphiniums out, but I've never seen these deep red flowers before. The captain's got a bee in his bonnet about flowers. He's been diggin' up everything in sight and packin' them in these pots from the conservatory. When we go back tomorrow he says he's goin' to plant them on the coverin' of soil that camouflages the headquarters dug-out. It's a nice idea that, cheer the fellows a bit. Wonder what it'll be like, goin' back? One thing's sure, it can't be worse than last time. That was bloody terrifyin'.

I'll never forget old Tom, never. He was the nearest to me when we were ordered over the top early that mornin'. Just a few yards in front of me when it started. The blastin' and screechin' of gun-fire and shells, all but deafened me, and the smell of high explosive and churned earth sickened me. I'd wished I was back in the trench with the rats and the mud. Then it happened. A thunderous explosion, I've never heard the like before, right on top of me. I couldn't see for the smoke but was sure I was hit. I lay flat and still. I was still breathin', so I wasn't dead, but I didn't feel anythin'. I'm paralysed! Oh God! No. When the smoke cleared I looked down at myself, and felt around. No pain, and I could move my arms and legs. I moved my head slightly. I was sure it was Tom in front of me, lyin' very still. I crawled towards him, started to turn him over, - then retched and vomited. It was Tom, with half his head blown off. To the left of Tom there was somethin' else, a torso, no legs, I couldn't see any arms or head either. I know I screamed. Then everythin' went quiet, until I heard low moanin'. I looked over. He was young, very young. He was sittin' up, little moans comin' from his lips, starin' into space, with an arm hangin' off.

I can't remember how I got back to the reserve trench but somebody told me what a lucky bastard I was. Out of fifty men, the youngster and me were the only ones to survive. The boy, they found out, was only sixteen. He'd lost his arm but not his life, and he'd been sent home.

I'm wishin', fillin' these pots with soil, it had been me sent home, even with an arm missin'. But then I remember there's been some good news after the slaughter of the last three months and I feel better. I'm sure I'll be goin' home soon, even if it's only a short leave. Roll on the day.


'There, it's done, thanks for your help Rose.' Emma, hands on hips, stretched and stood back, admiring the clean white sheets on the clothes line. 'There's nothing like lovely clean sheets blowing in the wind is there?' She smiled over at Rose, who was picking up the laundry basket. 'Mind, I would rather be hanging out Willie's shirts.' She sighed, 'Wonder what he's doing? Wonder if he's all right, getting enough to eat. Oh, sometimes I can't bear this waiting, I …'

'Come on pet.' Rose put down the basket and approached Emma. 'You're just a bit het up just now, what with your ma and pa away, and this of course,' she nodded down at Emma's bulge. 'You're certainly showing now, a lot more than last month. Have you heard back from him yet? I bet he's cock-a-hoop and – '

'But that's just it Rose, I haven't heard from him, don't even know if he got my letter.' The tears began to course down her face, as Rose put her arms around her and stroked her long dark hair.

Then Rose tightened her arms around Emma. 'You've got to stop this Em, you've got to try and think on the bright side or you'll make yourself ill. You should be proud of him, proud and happy. He was fit and well - well enough to go and fight, as he wanted to do.' She stopped for a moment looking down at her feet, then said 'You know Em, - sometimes I envy you.'

Emma looked up, grabbed a large handkerchief from her pocket, wiped her eyes then blew her nose. 'What - what do you mean, envy me? How can you envy me?'

'Well no, not really envy.' Rose looked again at her feet. 'It's just that, sometimes, I feel a bit ashamed.'

'Ashamed! What do you mean for heaven's sake?'

Rose laughed, an embarrassed little laugh, and looked at Emma.

'Well, you know, when Eddie was turned down for the front, because of that - that - little problem in his lungs, I felt a bit - ashamed.'

'How, Rose?'

'Oh, I don't know, but, well - especially when everywhere we walked, we saw these posters about Kitchener wanting you.'

'Well, you were daft,' Emma said, troubled by the sadness in Rose's eyes, but nonetheless wishing it had been Willie who'd been turned down.

'I suppose you're right. Anyway, let's forget the war.'

'Yes,' Emma said, linking her arm with Rose's. 'But how? That's what I want to know.'

'I know,' Rose said excitedly, turning to face Emma, 'I know exactly what'll cheer us up.'

'What?' Emma looked curiously into Rose's eyes, now bright with excitement.

'We'll go to the moving pictures, that's what!'

'Oh!' exclaimed Emma, looking at Rose doubtfully.

'Yes, Em, they're coming to the hall tonight and I've heard it's a great picture.'

'But I – I don't know Rose, I don't –'

'Of course you know, Em,' Rose said, grabbing Emma's arms. 'Don't be daft, it's a great Charlie Chaplin film and that new actress Mabel Normand's in it. It's called Mabel at the Wheel. It'll be a good laugh.'

'Well if you think – '

'Yes, I do think, and we're going – so come on.' She pushed Emma forward. 'Well, don't just stand there, we'll have to get moving.'

'All right then, I'm coming.' A smile played on Emma's lips, which quickly developed into a carefree laugh, as both girls ran into the house to get things organised before going along to the village hall.

'Yes, it's a jolly good idea, it'll cheer us both up a bit,' Emma admitted, as a sigh of relief escaped from between Rose's lips and she smiled.

The next day is quiet, with only the occasional explosion or short burst of machine gun fire, and Signaller-Corporal Willie Dunbar is sent forward to the observation post in front of Poelcapelle. It is almost five o'clock, and Willie sweeps the German line through binoculars from the roof of a shell-shattered farmhouse, when he spots a yellow cloud that is slowly drifting towards the British positions. A shiver, like iced water running down his spine, makes him tense, then he shouts to the captain, 'Look sir, look, take a look at this. There's something funny goin' on.' Something funny all right and he knows what it is. It's gas, that's what. Bloody gas. A wave of sickness comes up from his stomach. It's the bitter taste of bile, and Willie retches and spits it out.

Before he knows what's happening, the Hun lets rip and starts to pound the line. The captain yells back the orders and Willie leaps to the telephone to warn the guns and pass on the captain's orders. They've seen the yellow fog and don't hesitate in opening fire on all targets, right and left of the Poelcapelle road. But it's too late.

A high impenetrable wall of yellow-green smoke drifts down on the men in the trenches. None can run far, the German FK 96's come in as quickly as the smoke.

There's a crashing noise all around. Bedlam. Sounds of guns and men's screams. Willie looks again through the binoculars. He sees the men have no masks and they are coughing, gasping, choking; some foaming at the mouth. His stomach heaves. Suddenly, through the smoke and the pulverising shelling he sees Hamish and Ron. They're struggling out of the forward trench, in an attempt to make it to the reserve trench. 'Fools!' he yells, as he grabs a mask and zigzags towards them, the hissing and whistling of shells surrounding him. He bears down on them and flings them back into the trench. He can smell their sweat, feel their fear. The gas hasn't reached the bottom of the trench yet, and he thanks God. But he can see through the eye pieces of his mask, Ron is wearing his, and seems able to walk, but Hamish has no mask and looks like he's on his last legs. He whips off his own mask, and despite Hamish's weak protests he places it over his head. 'Lie low,' he orders him, 'and stay put.' Then he shouts to Ron, 'This is it mate, come on,' and he all but drags Ron the couple of hundred yards to the edge of the reserve trench, where their mates quickly haul them over the side.

'A mask, a mask,' he screams. 'Hamish is out there - quick.' He's given a mask and doesn't listen to the shouts, 'Leave him, he's done for.' He clambers over the side and someone shouts, 'Wait mate, wait, we're comin', hang on.' But he doesn't wait. He zigzags back again, ignoring the shells bursting around him. He's known Hamish for years, and he's damned if he's going to die in that hole. 'Damn and blast the Hun,' he shouts, as he reaches the trench. He's almost there, about to jump in, when a searing pain hits him in the shoulder and he falls into the trench. The pain is torture, like knives twisting in his flesh, but the gas is all around. He fumbles with the mask. He knows he's done for if he doesn't get it on.

Then Hell itself erupts. A shattering roar of fire above him and he feels the impact fall like hailstones on his steel helmet. He has the mask to his face when something strikes it from his hand. The muddy earth comes up before him like a black curtain. He tries to call out but he can only wheeze. Pain stabs at his throat and lungs. He feels his face smash into the mud ...

Emma walked in the field and gazed at the flowers. The colour of ripe strawberries. They had grown in abundance since she and Rose spotted them four years before. How often had she come here since that terrible summer of 1915?

Many times back then, she'd walked alone in that field, her hand around the neatly folded piece of paper in her pocket. She'd read the citation hundreds of times.

'Signaller-Corporal William Albert Dunbar: For conspicuous gallantry and devotion to duty.'

His medal, proudly displayed on the mantelpiece was pointed out to everybody who called.

The clouds had blotted out the sun that day. The ache, the longing, was a pain almost too terrible to bear.

She heard all about it later in the village, from Duncan, one of the three young men who came home. Three out of ten. Carnage he'd said. The other two weren't right in the head, wouldn't speak, couldn't. But Duncan did. He talked and talked, almost as if talking kept him sane. He told everyone about the butchering, the suffering, the pain, and she wept in her ma's arms, wishing to die. She prayed that Willie had died quickly, not slowly, obscenely. 'Why didn't they tell me?' She cried to her ma. 'I wanted to know, I wanted to know everything. Where's his body ma?' She asked. But nobody said, because nobody knew.

She'd cried tears of desolation then. But not today. Now the sun was shining in a clear blue sky. She sat, watching, as the warm summer breeze made the red poppies dance. The war was over, the world was new, it would never happen again - never.

'Mam, look.' She turned quickly. Little Will was running towards her, with Rose a few paces behind.

'Look how much we got.' Proudly he was holding an enormous bunch of blazing red blooms.

Smiling, she rose and walked to meet them, through the field of wild flowers, their scarlet blossoms waving on slender stems.

*Linda Cunniffe*

# No DSS!

Separated, divorced, mother of two,
surviving on Income Support.
Thank God for Lidl and charity shops,
without them perish the thought!

One hundred and twenty-five pounds a week,
includes Child Benefit too;
don't party or drink it or smoke it away,
but I know of people who do.

Problems begin when I need to move home,
good landlords want rent in advance.
Housing Benefit take eight weeks to pay,
so people like me stand no chance!

So I'm forced to choose from the dregs left behind;
they offer 'the house that Jack built,'
with its caved-in ceilings and woodworm to boot
and the walls have a strange sort of tilt.

The decorative order, bare wires everywhere,
plug sockets that work are so few,
and the musty stench of urine and poo,
are enhanced by the smell of mildew!

The carpets are worn threadbare and torn,
not a cupboard or shelf on the walls.
The gutters will strain when it's pouring with rain,
so we even get **free** waterfalls!

So this is my life now as an ex-wife
raising the kids on my own,
in 'the house that Jack built' with its walls, with their tilt,
and the carpets that welcome us home!

*Tania Oriol*

# Residential Friends

Head lice, head lice everywhere;
springtime beasties in your hair,
that drink your blood, then lay some eggs
and pass from hoods on coats on pegs!

'Won't jump or fly or swim,' they say,
but kids still catch them everyday.
Lotions, potions state and claim,
of how the lice can now be slain.

But blasted things became resistant;
Hell in hair still persistent.
Eggs live on and out pop MORE!
Now let's see who'll win this war!

Pregnant from the day they're laid.
Slip through nit-comb as a babe.
Can live on pillows in the home.
Will you have a lice-free zone?

Your only option – *'Shave all heads!'*
Change the pillows on your beds.
Little girls will go berserk!
Will this theory really work?

So to be a dad or mum,
your life with lice has now begun
and you like me will surely see,
this super louse – the human flea!

*Tania Oriol*

# The River

Enjoy it, for the last time. Pity, because it's a good walk this way, peaceful and pretty. But tonight is the last night, so enjoy the river and the grass with the trees on the banks. Feel that warm, soft breeze and the swirl of soft fabric on bare skin. We don't get many of these evenings, for all their talk of global warming, we just don't get the long hot summer evenings that I remember, and I'm not that old. Not sure at all that they know what they're on about. There's too much variation – which is what weather is, isn't it? I love the summer. People are beginning to smile at each other again. All through the winter I walked along here, and no one smiled or stopped for a chat. But the sun comes out; the heat starts building, and people slow down. They start to communicate again. Hot countries must have this all the time.

Hey, that guy, he was nice; I liked his smile, and his legs. Not seen him before. Isn't that just my luck? He looked local, like he was comfortable here. I could have done with some interest in my life, but it's not going to happen is it? Not with my lifestyle. Could do without the cyclists though. I don't mind the quiet ones, or the families with little kids, it's the head-down Lycra-clad-buttock brigade I can't stand. They've no respect.

I held the gate open for one guy last week. What are the chances of me walking up one shoulder of the hill, him cycling all the way up the Downs, and both of us arriving at the exact moment for me to be able to hold the gate open so he can sail through without dismounting? Amazing I call it. Did he? Did he heck! Never said thank you, not even an acknowledgement of my existence. It's all this fitness, it's a cult now. The new reality for the young, and the ones who want to be young. A warrior class. Is that why they feel superior to us lesser mortals? I'm not fit, but I'm not unfit either. I climbed that hill last week without any great effort. I don't make a fuss. But a sports goddess I'm not. When was the last time I really ran?

Oh not for a bus, oh no, that was for Danny. Wow, did I run that day! He'd have killed himself. He just got away. I only took my eyes off the little tyke for an instant and he bolted for the gate. Grabbed him back from the road and nearly got myself killed instead with the speed I was going.

I wonder where Danny is now? Poor little lad, all he needed was love and cuddles and time and patience and understanding and some rules. Mothering. That's all he needed, proper mothering. I nearly did it, almost turned him round, sorted out his behaviour and set him straight. Or am I just kidding myself even now? With his mum and dad, one stupid and the other with a cruel tongue, poor child, what chance did he really have? The way he was in school was certainly better, another few months and it would have become such a habit with him that it may have lasted. But I had to move didn't I? Off again once They found me. Didn't take Them long that time.

Aah, look at the swans. So elegant under the willows. Keep paddling you beauties. That's how I'd like to be: with a smooth, calm life, even if you do need to paddle hard. I'm not paddling though, I'm running scared, I can't stay, They just go on finding me and reminding me. So I pack and I move again to another new town, new job, and new kids. No time ever to settle, to get to know people and be part of an area. They are beginning to hurt me now: ten years and ten months with no home or husband, and certainly never kids of my own. No peace. Never able to relax.

Damn the post office. Of all the letters to deliver. They can't get it right just posting it from here to London on time, but one from Them, oh that one, they'll find me and deliver it. And they say there's a god - well he must be having a good laugh tonight.

I just get screwed up with guilt. I hate it. Why can't They be angry like normal parents? I know it was an awful accident, I know it wasn't really my fault, but it still happened when I was with her. I was there looking after Lucy. If only I hadn't had that glass of wine with my lunch. There was only one left in the bottle so I know I didn't have a lot. It was just the warmth and the peace. I can't have dozed for more than ten minutes because I heard the end of The Archers. Poor little girl, my poor Lucy. She won't be so little now. She'll never forget me, will she? I'll never forget her. The blood on her head. That cry. I've never heard terror like that. Don't want to ever again. God, the blood. Ten years and it still leaves me retching.

So They send me a birthday card again. Such a nice card with a happy, chatty letter, as if nothing bad had ever happened. Why can't They scream at me that if I hadn't fallen asleep I might have stopped that dog? I've always hated dogs like that; nasty yappy vicious dogs that you can't trust. I remember way back when Toby-dog attacked me. I've still got that scar on

- 52 -

my ear from when I was a girl. Mum said I only bent down to stroke him. I can only have been two.

But Will and Henrietta, They are just so kind and good it makes me hurt. Poor little Lucy. I think this is Their revenge, I'm sure of it now. At first I thought They were exceptionally good or brave people but now I'm not so sure. This is revenge, right enough, and it's far worse to carry this guilt. Talk about heaping coals of fire. I never took Them as being so clever. The happy family snap They put in each time They write to me. Will, Henrietta, pretty little Josephine and poor scarred Lucy with her hair always falling down over her blind eye. Please leave me alone … I didn't mean to do it, I only slept for ten minutes. I dozed, but I was there in the garden. I couldn't have stopped the dog crawling under the fence even if I'd been awake. I'm so sorry Lucy. I've paid enough in guilt. No. I'll never pay enough will I?

I'll have to move again, now They've tracked me down. They keep finding me, and They'll keep sending me letters. They'll never stop. I'm never going to escape am I? So clever, never a threat, never anything nasty, just a lovely birthday card, and a letter and snapshot of a happy family laughing in the sunshine. Greetings to their old nanny. How could anyone think ill of that family? It all sounds so loving, and forgiving and generous, but it's not is it? I know better. They find me. That's all They do, They only send me a letter, but They just let me know that They are there, and I can never forget. Never forget the guilt, the blood and screams and the snarls and the pulling, fighting the beast. He was shaking her. And she went quiet and so still, that he dropped her at last. Then the hours at the hospital when they struggled for Lucy, and the fight for her sight; oh, yes, I remember.

Look at the water here, it's peaceful and cool and still. Dark shadows. Silence and safety. They've found me now, but it will be the final time. This time I'll go where I want to go. I can escape you see. I can finally be free of all this.

*Sarah Chandler*

# Hopscotch

As I walked along memory lane, twilight from the setting sun bathed the world in a soft orange glow. Interplaying sunbeams radiated and flickered like candles in the wind. Narrow shafts of light moved in ever-changing patterns, playing tricks on the imagination, drawing me back to a different time, a different place. The houses looked taller and bleaker now. It was not how I remembered them.

Autumn leaves rustled, swirled in confusion on the pavement. The abandoned leaves of life briefly settled, then scurried along with the breeze seeking a place to rest. For some reason I glanced at my Rolex. It was 7.38 pm. If only time could stand still for a moment. If only I could grasp it in my hand .... Then a faint whisper, just audible, came into being. Yes, I can hear it now. It was the sound of a bygone age. A stone, bouncing, rolling, wobbling in innocent dance. A sound from the playground of childhood. Yes, of course, that was it. *Hopscotch.*

We used to chalk numbers from one to ten on the pavement. Some boys played the game just the once to try it out. Then all of a sudden it became too cissy. I wonder what Rita and the other girls thought of at that time. Maybe it was something in the rhyme they used to skip to. It came to me like a echo of a faraway hymn.

'*On a mountain stands a lady, who she is I do not know. So call in old Lilybelle, Lilybelle, Lilybelle, so call in old Lilybelle, we shall all fade away.*'

The breeze murmured again.

Clack, clatter, went the stone until it rested on a square. Suddenly, fleeting flickering phantoms came to life.

Sitting on the curb, I watched as the game progressed. I fancied Rita. Her flowing hair fascinated me as she hopped and skipped, showing off her skills. Mum said not to take any notice for her dad was only a dustman. Somehow I felt uncomfortable about that. She was arguing with Phoebe that the stone was touching the edge of the line. Maisy seemed disinterested and just wanted to get on with the game. Eventually it was settled with a grudging "miss-a-go".


On the fringes of this filmy fantasy, thunderclouds rolled across now darkening skies. Forked lightning fragmented the heavens, sending menacing shadows across the land. Nature rumbled as if in disgust at giving away its secrets. Ghostly images dimmed and faded. The voices from the fabric of time became silent again.

I sheltered from the storm in the shop around the corner. Rita was standing at the counter with a halfpenny in her hand.

'Packet of sherbet and a liquorice straw, please,' she was saying.

'What a beautiful sunny day,' remarked the old lady, handing her the sweets and ringing up the till. Rita turned, hesitated, then walked straight through me into the sun-light. It sent a shiver down my spine. Dumbfounded, I followed her through the door into another reality.

I had no shadow. Mortal but invisible. My watch had stopped at 7.38 pm. The wheels of time jammed. I called out to Rita but there was no response. I was an observer trapped in time.

Flights of fancy and fear entered my thoughts: of parallel universes with dimensions undefined. Drifting ghosts roaming the ether, searching through a tapestry of forgotten faces. The faces of my childhood friends who I used to play with and share my innermost secrets. Streets empty of cars, bringing the boundaries of home closer to the heart. It was strangely comforting.

As I passed the prefabs a lone dog barked. It was aware of my presence.

A life force without form, an existence that was not complete. A spirit in limbo, reliving the past? I wasn't sure. Then a bizarre thought occurred to me. Could I change the future for poor Rita? The Tarot of the ages was soon to deal her a cruel hand.

Patsie, the bookmaker's runner, was still keeping watch on the corner. It was a Saturday afternoon. In the distance boys were playing French cricket in the road. Neighbours were milling around in groups gossiping about the new Woolworth store that had opened at Clapham Junction. 'How posh,' someone was saying, hands awry in mocking stance. 'You'd have to be lah-de-dah to shop in a place like that.'

When I caught up with Rita, she had joined her friends doing wall stands in the alley that overlooked the woodyard. Alfie and Tom were trying to guess what colour knickers the girls were wearing and showing off.

'Where's Johnny?' enquired Rita, looking puzzled. 'He was here just a minute ago.' Her eyes scanned the shady niches that dotted the alley. 'I suppose he's hiding from his mum. He knows he's in for a telling off for taking me to the pictures. We watched *Old Mother Riley* at the Super Palace together.'

'I wish my boyfriend would take me to the pictures,' whined Phoebe, pushing off the wall with her feet. 'You don't know how lucky you are.'

'Is Johnny in?' Rita was asking, all dolled up in her high heels and lipstick.

'Leave my son alone,' was the terse reply. The door slammed. It was the year of the coronation, 1952. Battersea Park fun-fair had just opened. With a half-a-crown crown tucked away in my pocket we sneaked off. Distant music from the merry-go-round quickened our pace. Strains of *The Loveliest Night Of The Year* filtered through the night air. Round and round went the melody, exciting the imagination, drawing us like a magnet. Holding hands, we began to run.

'Johnny, I've a crush on you,' she suddenly blurted out, pulling me back.

'Snap!' I answered. 'Race you to the park gates. There's a candyfloss stall there.'

'Let's try the big dipper first, Johnny,' she pleaded, clip-clopping behind me breathless with excitement.

The big wheel slowly jolted and jerked its way upward as the seats filled. We had reached the highest point before the spin. On top of the world. Harmonious laughter and music filtered up from the glittering stalls below.

The occasional 'Roll up, roll up, everyone's a winner' came to the fore. Rita was pointing out the houses on the skyline.

'Look!' she said, 'We live over there! Can you see the top of our church? When we get older we'll have a home of our own.'

Fact and fantasy merged again. I found myself walking in the rain towards the alleyway. I sat there in the silence of the night listening to the past, trying to work out how to save Rita from her fate. It happened on a Sunday. I'm sure of that. As I looked down the narrow path, a faint glow drew me towards the wood yard. There in the corner was the renowned fortune teller's charabanc, just how I remembered it.

Gypsy Rose Lee was gazing into the crystal. The light from the tilly lamp picked out hidden treasures. All around were the trappings of her trade. Beads and charms glinting of gold and silver hung from the ceiling. Luxurious curtains framed the small leaded windows.

Peering into the mists of the crystal she made contact. 'Your aura tells me you are a projection from the future. You were the boy that lived at number 39. Heed my warning! Don't meddle with destiny. It has already been written. No one can change the wheels of time. Let it be, or take the consequences.' Her eyes reflected the wisdom of the ages. But she knew I would try. Rita meant a lot to me.

'I have lost my attendance book,' Rita was complaining to Johnny. Maisy was proudly showing off hers. It was full of stamps depicting biblical scenes.

'I must find it,' tears welled up in Rita's eyes.

'Don't worry my dear, I have plenty spare at the vicarage,' coaxed the Reverend, who was hovering nearby. 'Come along with me, I shall replace it for you.'

Sunday School had just finished. I had to make a move soon. Maybe it was possible to influence Johnny's thoughts by telepathy. We were of the same mind, my younger self in fact. It should be possible. If only I could induce a slight change in his behaviour at the critical moment.

This was the day of temptation. The day an innocent would pay the price of trust. As the Reverend was leading her away towards the church house Johnny suddenly called out, 'Rita, I've just remembered! You left it at Maisy's last week.'

Darkness unleashed its mantle. The spinning wheel of time tumbled out of control. Approaching horizons clashed in confusion. The past was forced to change course. Parallel universes were in the making.

Above, clouds of gilded silver raced across a full moon. Foreboding mist glided menacingly through the churchyard. Cauldrons of chaos reflected from stained-glass windows. Distorted images flared and faded. A faint whisper, just audible, came into being. Rita was calling to me from the other side of reality, pleading with me to return. Something had gone wrong. Had I intervened too early? Fate had brutally shifted. Rita should have lived.

It must have been the gipsy's curse! Or was it? Then a dim recollection came to mind - yes I remember now, it was written somewhere - a newspaper headline. 'Vicar rapes girl then hangs himself.'

Gradually a silent entity formed over a gravestone. There in its shadow, a faded inscription.

*Rita Collings*
*Died in childbirth*
*7 June 1953*

I needed to go back.
Time: 7.38 pm.

**Ron Nicola**

# Runner Beans & Mint Sauce
## A Monologue for TV

**Scene**: Reg, aged somewhere between 65 and 70, is in shirtsleeves and old brown cord trousers. The clothes are old, his gardening gear, and are splattered across the front with reddish brown smears. He is digging in the back garden of a typical suburban semi-detached house, which sports a small flower garden to the front whilst the back is a patch of grass with flower borders around the four sides. He is using a well-worn spade and digs in ordered rows across the left-hand flower border, the lawn in the centre and then the far flower border. Almost half the garden is already dug and is neat, level and devoid of any grass, weeds or flowers.

*(Reg stops digging and thumps the spade blade first into the dug soil. He picks up a pint glass from a pile of bricks set a few feet behind him on the left and drinks deeply. He replaces the glass, spits into his palms and resumes digging).*

REG You just can't beat shandy on a beautiful September day like today. "Oils the spade" as they say.

Just look at that.

*(He pauses and nods at the neat newly dug soil).*

Now, what can be nicer than that I ask you? You don't even need to plant anything, just keep the soil turned over. Beautiful!

Mind you, women don't see it the same, do they? Always wants flowers in neat rows: tidy and weed free. It gives colour, I'll grant you - *she* loved colour, especially red, but why not carrots and onions? A few lettuces and spuds. What's nicer than them small early spuds where the skin just rubs off in your fingers, eh?

And mint sauce. Every garden should have mint sauce growing, spring cabbage and mint sauce. Hah!'

*(Reg grins hugely at the thought).*

Who cares if it's a bit untidy? What did *she* call it? "Invasive!" Bloody silly word that - what's wrong with: "abundant"? "bountiful" or even "rampant"?

*(Reg sniffs loudly and carries on digging in silence, picking out the occasional weed or piece of grass. At the end of the row he stops and rubs his hands across his stomach and down onto his trousers.).*

Course I grew 'em all on the allotment. In the early days, when the kids were little and pennies were short. *She* was glad enough for all the stuff I grew then. Not only that, she could score a few Brownie points with that stuck-up sister of hers by keeping her in spuds and cabbages. Aye, in those days she could put up with a few mallyshags and slugs easy enough.

Things started to go downhill when the kids grew up and left home though. Oh, we let 'em have lettuces, beans and the like, but it felt as if they only took it to please me. Okay, my stuff had a bit of dirt still on it whereas Tesco's was washed spotless - sanitised you could say. You could see them peering down into the leaves for "wildlife" as they called it.

Best allotment up on the embankment, mine was. Everybody said so. But *she* wouldn't come up, would she? Most wives did. Some brought a flask and homemade cake. But not her. "Don't like the company you keeps up there," she'd say.

Then it got worse. *She* started timing me.

"Where you been all this time?" *(He sardonically mimics).*

"You're not going up there *again*?" *(He mimics).*

God, it got my goat.

But it wears a feller down, all that nit-picking. Slowly but surely I cut back on the hours. And weren't the weeds glad?

But *she* didn't let up did she? Oh no. She even piled it on heavier and heavier.

Then one day she actually came up. I nearly pronged me foot with shock. But she only wanted to bend my ear about leaving her on her own all day. Crikey, she did let on.

Everyone was embarrassed. Old Charlie and Pete Pettigrew didn't know where to look. Billy Gosden nearly choked on his pipe, and Ken Brewer just packed up and went home.

I tried reasoning with her, but that just wound her up even more. When she burst into tears I just put my tools away in the shed and went home. I know when I ain't going to win.

But it was like the sun going out.

I never went back, and resigned from the allotment committee. Thirty-three years! And I had some pretty good stuff coming on too.

The sun went out on us at home too.

What was there to talk about? Alan-bloody-Titchmarsh and his poncy flower drifts with "structure" and "form"? No bloody fear!

I was better off on me own upstairs with a bit o' peace an' quiet than being told endlessly what "Alan" says.

Oh, I dug her flowerbeds for her, but she had to plant her precious marigolds, lobelia and gazenias - whatever they are. She tried to make me plant 'em for her, but I dug me heels in. Ha! No pun intended.

If we got to have flowers let her plant 'em I say.

I mean, even a few runners against the south-facing fence would have been pretty, and useful too. But no. Vegetables would "despoil the balance and lower the tone".

Alan doesn't do it, and he wrote the Gospel didn't he?

I suggested we split the back garden into two. I'd have the far end – down there.

(*He points to the patch already dug over*).

And *she* could have the bit nearest the house. Seemed fair enough to me.

(*Reg sighs deeply*)

We didn't speak for a week after that.

God, she could be a miserable cow at times and she took sulking into a different league.

No - I didn't get a veggie plot. In fact I ended up having to mow and de-weed the grass. Honestly, you couldn't really call it a lawn could you?

I hate mowing grass; except perhaps the path between my allotment and Dennis Vicary's. An' I could keep that down with the shears. But, of course,

I hadn't got my allotment any more had I? Made me loathe that bloody lawn even worse. Rubbed it in, see.

(*Reg stops digging and fetches his glass of shandy again*).

Hot work digging when the sun's out. The secret's to only take small spits each time, see. No point breaking your back.

(*He swallows hungrily*).

Hah - that's better.

Now for the trench. Runners will go across here just right. They'll screen off the lower half where I'll have cabbages, onions, marrows and the mint sauce.

Runners are hungry buggers you know. Needs lots of goodness under them, so the trench will need to be wide, and deep.

Some folks have an open trench all winter and sling in all the household bits and pieces. Spud peelings, the rough old cabbage and lettuce leaves, and the like. By the following spring they have a good layer of well rotted compost for the beans. Of course, others like manure whilst some swear by pellet feed.

Me? I'm trying something new. You see, I won't get enough veg' matter to have an open trench now I'll be on my own, and I don't fancy dragging bags of manure through the house.

No, I'm mindful of what *she* kept on about when she was on her herbaceous border project, "If you don't plant anything you won't get nothing coming up." But let's face it - there are some things that get planted that are better for not coming up.

(*Reg winks and nods to himself.*)

Yes, runners seem right for here. The flowers are pretty too. Bright red. *She* always kept on about having flowers.

(*Reg spits into his palms and rubs them together*).

Must be getting on.

(*He starts digging and piles the new earth up onto the already dug patch*)

**John Vallender**

# Spiritus Sancti

My mind is the wind
Ever reaching
My blood, the ocean
Ever flowing.
My soul, the flame
Ever burning.
My body, the soil
Ever fertile.

I am the four elements combined,
Bound together by God's hands,
And when my time is done,
To them, I shall return.

*Joe Strange*

# Philosophy of Knowledge

See me?
Yes you do.
Know me?
No you don't.

You pretend to listen
To what I say.
You nod in punctuation
In all the right places,
But you don't follow me.

You see the world
In black and white,
Life as one straight road
Between two points.

A piano's keys
Are these two colours,
Yet its concertos
Are complicated

And the straightest road,
Is often the loneliest,
For it is the least tread.

To some,
Ugly is beautiful
And beauty
Is only skin deep.

Does that make
The Devil awe-inspiring
And God shallow?

See me?
Yes you do
Know me?
No you never will.

I am the torch
That ignites the fire
Of comprehension.

I provoke you
To ask questions,
But expect you
To seek the answers.

See me?
No you don't.
Understand me?
How can you understand,
That which you cannot see?

*Joe Strange*

# The Scorecard

V r o o m.

An aeroplane roars over the Village Green, missing the church and skimming the clump of trees on the top of the hill above Farmer Millsom's hen farm, scattering the hens and frightening his black and white dog.

'A Spitfire,' shouts Bobby. He is sure it is.

'A Hawker Hurricane,' says Smith Junior, the smartie.

'No, a Spitfire…'

'I tell you it's a Hurricane. You only have to look at the tips of the wings. And there's a big airscoop under the engine… I know. My brother's a pilot, he tells me all about planes.'

'Well, it's one of ours, anyway…'

It's summer holidays and we're playing cricket on the Recreation Ground, Bobby and me, Colin Lamplin, the postman's son, and Minnow, the little boy. The girls, Lizzie and Lydia, are fielding and sometimes they are allowed to bowl their sissy under-arm ones that are easy to hit. And Smith Junior, the smartie, of course. He's always the captain of the other side. And it's his ball.

I knew the aeroplane was one of ours. In my Biggles book all the German planes have black crosses on the wings. But I don't say. Smith Junior knows more about everything than anyone else and I didn't want to make Bobby feel more rotten than he did already.

'How do you know?' I ask.

Bobby says, 'Ours have three circles, red, white and blue, one inside the other, on the wings and on the sides. I knew it was one of ours. Anyway, it's gone now, whatever it was.'

'A Hawker Hurricane,' says Smith Junior, the smartie.

It certainly had. All we got was a glimpse, playing cricket in the sunshine, as it roared in one end of the village and out over Farmer Millsom's hen farm at the other. Gone in a split second.

'It was very low,' I say. Smith Junior says it was 'on a mission.'

'Anyway, if your brother is so clever,' says Bobby, 'why isn't he up there in the sky fighting the Germans?'

'He is.'

The hens are just gathering themselves together in little groups and starting to peck at the ground again and Farmer Millsom's dog has come out of hiding. Farmer Millsom is standing outside the hen house, hands resting on his hips, looking up into the sky like Biggles' Commanding Officer does waiting for his aeroplanes to return.

'I expect he's swearing now,' Bobbie says. 'Like my grown-up brother does. You are allowed to swear when an aeroplane frightens your chickens or your motorbike breaks down.'

Dad had said lots of aeroplanes were flying over our village because of the Battle of Britain and we were defending our country against the Germans, in Kent and Sussex, near where we went on holidays to Mrs Snell's Guest House in Hastings.

Dad says we are 'fighting for our lives.' It is that important and he listens to the man on the wireless every night to 'keep up with things.' He tells how many planes have been shot down, ours and theirs. Like our cricket scores.

'Yesterday we got 57 and they got 32. The day before it was 66 and they only got 23...'

Dad says that sometimes the planes will be flying over our village, like today. 'That's probably what he was doing. Searching for a German to shoot at.'

Mum says we must run indoors and hide under the table the next time we see an aeroplane. 'Promise me, you will?'

I promise, but only half-heartedly. 'I still want to see our aeroplanes chase off the Germans,' I say.

Mum's about to do some scolding. 'And getting riddled with bullets?'

'What's riddled, Mum?'

In Dad's pub, Mr Jiggins, the roadsweeper, had told Dad how he had seen several aeroplanes chasing each other. He stopped and leant on his broom and watched them until Mr Trendle the roly-poly policeman had told him to 'get down before yer 'ead gets blown off.'

He did get down under the hedge by the Little Piddlington Road and stayed there 'til they had gone even though he was in a nettle patch.

'It was a dogfight,' said Mr Blenkinsop the village butcher, who is like Smith Junior, the smartie, but grown up. He also knows everything. 'That was a dogfight,' he repeated in case some in the pub hadn't heard. 'A dogfight.'

'Looked like aeriplanes to me,' Mr Jiggins had said. He'd seen nothing like it before. 'Anyway, them nettles is good for yer joints. I don't mind getting a bit of a stingin'.'

'I hope Mrs Snell is alright,' I say to Mum. 'Dad says the Battle of Britain is happening over her boarding house every day. I hope she isn't being bombed. And the man who sells ice creams on the pier. I want one of his strawberry ones when the war's over.'

Bobby says, 'Come on...who's going to bat first? Toss for it.'

He is nearly always our best batter. I only got 11 last time and Bobby got 20 but we still lost to Smith Junior's side. Smith Junior got 33 but he made the rules up as he went along and said he was still in when he was out.

Minnow tells us that a German aeroplane had crashed in Little Piddlington. It had gone straight into a haystack. His Dad told him although no-one else had seen it.

'Hasn't your Dad got a bit of the aeroplane?' asks Smith Junior, the smartie. 'Everyone gets a bit of a German plane when it crashes. As a prize.'

Minnow says his Dad didn't have time to get a prize; he was cycling to work. 'Anyway, there was a policeman standing by it. They always put a policeman by crashed German planes in case Hitler's in it. Then he arrests him.'

Smith Junior thinks Minnow's Dad should have a bit of the plane to prove it. 'Or we might think he made it up.'

Minnow had a good point, I thought. Anyway, I didn't want to pick on him, he was only little. It wasn't his fault his Dad hadn't pinched a bit of the German aeroplane, with Hitler sitting in it, in a haystack.

'Heads,' calls Bobby and heads it is. 'We're batting.'

'Can I go in first,' says Colin Lamplin, the postman's son. 'I haven't been an opener for ages.' Then it's Bobby's turn, then mine and Minnow's next.

Henry, the lanky boy, is going to bowl. He bowls proper ones, not sissy under-arm ones like the girls when they have a go. Proper over-arm ones that are really hard to hit. I hope I get loads and loads of runs and we win.

Bobby gets 35 including two sixes that go over the hedge and into the road. Colin gets lots more. I get 15 and then we skittle out Smith Junior's side.

'We won, Dad. We won.'

Dad seems very pleased. 'How do you know, son?' he asks. 'It's only just come on the wireless… the Germans have pulled out of the Battle of Britain. Yes, we won.'

That night the sky glows red, to the East, towards London.

'The Blitz has started,' says Bobby, next morning.

Colin says his Mum was in tears. 'My big sister is up in London… Mum thinks she might be bombed.'

Smith Junior, the smartie, says it's nothing. Our aeroplanes will get it sorted. Like they did in the Battle of Britain. 'Come on,' he says, 'Give you a game of football. I want to beat you lot.'

*Richard Holdsworth*

## *Controlled* Freak

'You're so bloody *perfect*, there's no living with you! You're a freak!' Brian slammed the front door behind him. The force of the closure shook the windows and brought the neighbours to theirs. White-faced and shaking, Adele watched him wrench open his car door, launch himself inside, reverse at speed to the road, and over-accelerate away. It was the last she ever saw of him.

The shock of his statement was quickly followed by anger. How dare he! She picked up the newspaper he'd thrown at her, ripped off a page, screwed it into a ball and threw it at their wedding photograph on the sideboard. 'You bastard!' She snatched at another page, and another, and hurled them at his smirking face until the shredded paper was used up.

'Take that, and that, and that!'

Caught up in the passion to destroy him, she cast around for a heavier object. His pipe, his horrible smelly pipe! Plucking it from its singed wooden wall rack, she threw it hard against the picture and scored a hit. The frame crashed to the floor, still intact. Her self-control vanished and she stamped on it with her high heels, splintering the glass and defacing the photograph. At last she had him. Shaking the picture free from the mess, she looked at his disfigured image.

'That'll teach you, you selfish, self-centred, conceited bastard!' she shouted aloud. 'For ten years I've wanted to hit back when you've complained, and black your eyes when you've given younger women the "come on" when we've been out together.' Ripping the photograph in two, she held onto the piece picturing herself. Single for far too long, marrying a man eight years younger, anticipating happiness and babies, her innocence and love radiated from the print. The memory brought a pain to her chest, an almost physical lump in her throat. There'd been no babies. Brian had changed his mind, *he'd* become her infant, demanding her entire attention.

She threw the torn picture down in disgust and went to the kitchen, grinding the glass splinters into the carpet as she passed. Filling the kettle, she caught sight of the party invitation pinned neatly in the top right-hand corner of the message board.

'Sorry,' Brian had said, 'I'm playing snooker that night.' How many invitations had been "regretfully" turned own because of his golf, his fishing and his late nights at the office? She'd persuaded herself that a younger man must be given his head occasionally, and welcomed him home with presents, and his favourite meals. The whistling kettle shut off her thoughts and she reached for the bone-china teapot. Before she met him, Brian had only ever made tea with a tea-bag in a stained mug. She had made a point of introducing him to the finer things in life. She let the tea brew for the required six minutes before pouring, then took the cup and saucer on a melamine tray embellished with daisies and poppies up to the bedroom, kicking the newspaper balls with relish as she passed.

'Damn him!' The tears of her anger streaked her face, leaving salt trails, and her hair had become dishevelled. Automatically she put her face back to rights. Years of striving to always appear at her best for him was second nature to her. Picking up her cup, she went to stand by the bed to drink it. She smoothed one hand over a pillow. His pillow. Grinding her teeth, she recalled the nights she'd lain awake waiting to hear him come home, lying perfectly still with the covers his side of the bed turned down in a welcome, only to have him turn his back on her, or exclaim that he was tired. And how, by the next morning she'd always forgiven him and brought him a cup of tea in bed. Her hands trembled with the injustice of it all and she laid her cup aside, unwanted.

She'd fashioned her life around him, bent to his every whim, become totally controlled by him, tried to be everything he could possibly want in a wife. Now he'd thrown it all in her face. Ten years of pent up frustration escaped her in a terrible scream.

It had been a year since Brian had left, a year in which she'd re-built her shattered life. Ten years of ministering to his every demand had prepared her well for her new venture.

From the vantage-point behind the lounge net curtains, Adele watched her departing guests getting into their BMW. Good, now she could change the sheets and clean the room in readiness for her next B & B booking.

She entered the bedroom, sniffing suspiciously for tell-tale signs of banned smoking, and straightened the sign on the door. She pulled off the sheets and sighed. Signs of love-making made her feel jealous with longing to be loved herself, and at the same time repelled her with the thought of others making love in her beds. She clamped her teeth tightly and disrobed the pillows. Sure enough, lipstick stains on the slip where the woman had slept, and a powerful smell of after-shave on his. These days, she thought, you couldn't even trust people with expensive cars to wash properly before they went to bed. Distastefully, she continued to strip the bedding. She began to remake it again, from the mattress up, tucking in the sheets tightly so that not one wrinkle appeared, fitting the plump pillows into lightly starched cases and pulling the broderie anglaise frill taughtly, so that it stood out like a little halo around the pure white mound. With ease, she carefully stuffed the down-filled duvet into its freshly ironed cover, pushing the ends of the calico covering precisely into the corners, before she flicked it into the air, letting it settle softly over the bed, like a great white swan landing gently on a lake.

On her hands and knees, she inspected the floor beneath the bed for any dropped tissues and, finding none, she put her white cotton gloves back into her apron pocket. She opened the drawers in the dressing-table, all empty today, thank goodness. She wouldn't be obliged to go the post office and spend unnecessary money returning forgotten items, generally used underwear. She set to and vacuumed the floor, polished all the surfaces including the dark wooden headboard, until she could see her faint reflection in it. She closed and opened the curtains, so that they fell into the ordered folds that she'd so carefully moulded. She wished people wouldn't yank them back. If parted carefully with the pulley-cord, it was like an eye-lid opening to see what treasures lay beyond. For a brief moment she gazed down onto the bright green grass, mown end to end to echo the stripes she'd seen in the gardening advertisements. Multi-coloured dahlias hung their flowers over the lawn borders, neatly kept in place with unseen green corrugated plastic edging, the patio table and chairs, still damp from their daily scrub, already blindingly white in the early morning sunlight.

She turned and straightened the mirror. Just a fraction out of true, but offensive none-the-less. Reflected in the glass, she noticed the bed-side books had been disturbed. Checking that the bible hadn't been used for scribbling telephone numbers, she placed the three books in a fan so that each showed precisely the same amount of cover, and positioned the house rules and meal-time schedule, in its hard shiny plastic cover, prominently on top of the cabinet.

There, all done. She leaned against the door and looked with approval at the completed picture. Nobody could ask for more.

Passing through the hall, she noticed that the visitors' book had been used. Curiously, she bent to read…

Lovely welcome, fantastic food, ideal home,
*Almost too perfect!*

**Jean Russell-Parnell**

# A Photo on the Shelf

There's a photo on the shelf
And when I'm by myself,
I hold it and I brush away a tear.
Although I know you've gone
It isn't very long,
Before I feel your presence very near.
I talk to you for hours
As I rearrange the flowers,
And I know you know, the hurting that I feel.
I miss you oh so much,
I miss your tender loving touch,
And I wish that I could see you once for real.

There's a photo on the shelf
And when I'm by myself,
I think of all the things that I regret.
Did I tell you that I love you?
That I know you loved me too,
Did we argue very much? I quite forget.
Did you think I didn't care,
The times I wasn't there?
Did you know that others needed me as well?
Will the guilt I feel each day
Ever go away? Or will I live forever with this hell?

When I think of what we had
I don't need to feel this sad,
I think of all the good times that we shared.
I remember all the fun,
And all the things we've done,
Deep down I know, you know how much I cared.
I don't need to feel this gloom,
When I'm alone inside this room,
And searching for the soul inside myself.
It's just the passing of the hours,
The fragrance of the flowers.
And the photo of you, there, upon the shelf.

*Anne Hooker*

# Coronation Clock Tower

One hundred years upon this spot I've stood
Heralding the reign of Edward the Seventh
With hope of peace and mounting wealth
Severely dimmed by ignorance and greed.

Built of granite, brick and glass
My tower enfolds a clock and silent bell
Measuring time by night and day
And charting strangers on their way.

Life, though, has not been always dull
Coping with elemental change and seismic threat
Has tested my mettle to the full
And given hope of better days.

Ships I've seen, passing day and night
With multifarious cargoes filled
Surviving temperamental seas and heaving winds
Their destination to achieve.

The years have passed with monarchs come and gone
And Britain's role in history changing fast
Whilst for good or ill I have played my part
As silently my vigil I pursue.

*Paul Lendon*

# Not Trying to Cause a Big S-Sensation

But I'm talking 'bout my generation.

Yes, us, this year's crop of newly-fledged OAPs, those of us born in 1940.

We're new and we're different. We are the pensioners with "attitude" so are you ready for us? We were born *during* the War, one huge difference between us and our predecessors. Of course we remember certain aspects of that time, after all we were the Blitz Babies, but we don't go around boring the pants off everyone by recounting the details of every doodlebug that ever dropped out of the sky. We've forgotten the ration books, the hand-me-down clothes, the margarine queues and working for three farthings a day. So what if we *didn't* see a banana until we were fourteen?

We were the first generation that missed out on National Service but only just. If you were born in 1939 you were called up but 1940 meant you were safe. Thankfully then we weren't put in the tender hands of the Armed Forces to "make men" out of us. So we missed the troubles in Cyprus and the very strong possibility of getting in the way of a stray EOKA bullet. You won't hear us preaching about how good compulsory National Service would be, taking crime off the streets and so on and so on. We escaped and we're pleased about that.

We've actually got a life.

Modern inventions don't bother us. We've had mobile phones for years, long before the spotty, tattooed and body-pierced kids of today. Some of us can even use predictive text but it does go against the grain somewhat. We're computer literate and we know a spreadsheet when we see one, we can e-mail and surf the Internet. Thousands of us are still working because the more switched on employers realise we are capable of speaking English, composing letters and adding up a few simple figures without spell checks and calculators. We are old enough to actually be bright, shining beacons in the dull grey workplaces, head and shoulders above the slouching, monosyllabic twenty-somethings. Their basic education either never existed or has been long forgotten, ("know what I mean like, ennit?"). Some might stereotype us as Grumpy Old Men but we are much more than that. We are vibrant, virile, and if there's the occasional failure in that department then there's always Viagra.

It's being said that 2005 will be declared as a vintage year for OAPs, earthy, full-bodied, with a surprising hint of sophistication. Sixty-five is just a number and we don't care. Stuff your Nanny State! We never had a nanny when we were young and we don't need one now. The same goes for your special concessions! We don't mind paying full prices in most cases, especially to watch our local football teams. The clubs need all they can get and most of us are not too badly off. So, turnstile attendants, don't give us your pitying little smile and don't mention our special rates. Take the cash and shut up.

As for bus passes, what the hell use are they? What is a bus anyway? Most of us wouldn't recognise one and haven't travelled that way since we were kids. We rode motorbikes in the 50s and drove cars from the 60s onwards. Buses just make overtaking difficult for us in our Mercs and BMWs. And how long do they take to get anywhere with their ancient spluttering engines? They're uncomfortable and they don't even have conductors any more. They're O.K for school kids with I-Pods sticking out of their ears and ladies with shopping bags.

We do admit we've been taking the government's fuel allowance. Well we're not quite *that* civic minded. I mean 200 quid for doing nothing is hard to turn down and the cash comes in handy, helping us keep up with the advances in technology on the golf course. A new driver these days costs every bit of that and more. As for using the money to buy fuel, don't be silly. We were brought up in draughty houses with icicles *inside* the windows and central heating a long way into the future. Hypothermia? Forget it, that's not for us. We're tough old buggers and don't really feel the cold but, thanks Mr Blair, keep sending the cheques.

Everyone these days is on a health kick. But look around your local gym and you'll see silver-haired, bright-eyed old codgers, all born in 1940, and managing, well almost, to keep pace with the far younger poseurs with their Nike headbands and fancy stopwatches. We are fitter and stronger than our predecessors.

Some say we even look younger, well not all of us of course but Cliff Richard, 65 this October, seems to doing OK. All right, perhaps he's not a good example but the icons of our youth have not been surpassed have they? Where is the next Elvis or John Lennon (another 1940 boy)? Who's taken the place of James Dean, Marlon Brando or Marilyn Monroe?

Growing up, we ate healthy, nourishing food, no Big Macs and French Fries and now we enjoy good restaurants and fine wines. OK we smoked cigarettes, everybody did, and some of us paid the price, but we are the first generation to benefit from modern surgery and all the wonderful new drugs. We are the Simvastatin Kids, anti-cholesterol pill takers to a man and not forgetting the single aspirin a day. Our hearts have been bypassed, our arteries fixed, our eyes have been lasered and if the odd hip or knee packs up we just get a replacement.

We will live forever.

So yes I'm talking 'bout my generation', as in the song by The Who, but forget the line "Hope I die before I get old," because *we* didn't. We're still here and we're here to stay.

Get used to the idea.

Instead take notice of another great line in that song and,

"Why don't you all f-fade away?"

*Ken Baker*

Extract from
# Castle in the Sea

Moonshine fell into the apartment, spotlighting the pianist as he bent his head over the keyboard letting the blood of a great composer. The piano was at the heart of Louis's room and Peter was striking the heart-strings. Encircled by shadows, he straddled the stool while his fingers let flow the life-blood of Beethoven. Louis fancied that in the moonlight Peter resembled a classical god hewn from marble - the Apollo Belvedere perhaps.

'I love these bagatelles,' said Peter, coming to the end of a piece. He started another and the blood came thicker. Although a book of music lay open in front of him, he was not reading from it as the light was too dim.

Louis's mind wandered off into a world of dreams. He was still dreaming when Peter stopped playing. The music had streamed out of the room onto the verandah; it had streamed out across the city, up into the hills and towards the harbour. And Louis had not heard it. But now it had ended, he was awakened by the silence that serenaded him. And he knew the time had come to ask an awkward question.

Peter had stridden away from the piano. Still orbed in moonshine, he stood between Louis and the cocktail cabinet. His fingers - Louis resisted an impulse to twist his tongue between them - curled round the neck of a decanter. Brandy gurgled into one glass, then another. The noise commanded Louis's attention more than Beethoven had. Peter held out a drink to him. Louis's hand flew up in response, but reached past the glass and gripped Peter's forearm. With his other hand, he took the drink and put it down. A concourse of blue veins threaded the white flesh of Peter's wrist, and unable to resist a new impulse, Louis plugged his lips to it and let them quaver on the pulse of his friend's life.

'You know,' said Louis, releasing his hold and embarrassed by his own show of passion, 'what I must ask you, don't you?' The serenade at once plunged into dissonance. A cloud cloaked the moon. Wordlessness darkened the room. 'I must ask you,' he blundered on, 'what my father did for you. Why does he have such a hold on you?'

Perhaps the question was indelicate. He half wished he had not asked it. Nothing must jeopardise their relationship. Peter was the foundation of his new life. The future lay in Peter's hands and must not be set aside as lightly as a glass of brandy.

He probed the night for the cause of Peter's silence. In the harbour, the growl of a motor-launch whirred above the lapping of waves. In the hills, the yapping of a dog irrupted on the chatter of cicadas.

Peter picked up his glass and drank. Louis heard the glass scrape the table, heard it clink against teeth, heard the spirit sucked up and swilled down, heard again the scrape on the table. Then there was a shuffle as Peter sat down cross-legged at Louis's feet. Still he did not speak.

And now the cloud divested the moon and light straked the floor. Surely, Louis should not have asked that question. If only he could see Peter's eyes! They would provide an answer even while the voice denied it. But gloom hung like a veil. Moonbeams might collect on Peter' knees, flood along his shins, silver hairs where they sprouted between the tops of his socks and the bottoms of his trouser-legs, but his face lay enshrouded in shadow.

'What's the matter?' asked Louis. 'Won't you say something?'

The moon grew big - verily varicose - and looked as though it might bash through the verandah. Already it was transfusing its light into the deepest veins of the apartment, revealing alcoves, discovering bookcases and cabinets, and at last illuminating Peter's features.

'All right,' sighed Peter, unable to hide any longer. 'Your father - well, he paid my school-fees.'

Louis gasped. He did not understand. What new mystery was this that draped Apollo even at the moment when moonlight disrobed him? He stepped out onto the verandah. He needed to think. He needed to breathe. The heat of the night was suffocating. The moonlight scorched his face. The poinsettias that lined the balustrade - so colourful earlier in the afternoon - had shrivelled. The harbour looked white-hot. It seemed as though the moon was devouring the world and he wondered if he were going mad.

***Tony Pook***

# Yesterday and Today

Yesterday
I looked out from a sun-happy garden
Over the beautifully disordered stack of multi-coloured houses
Standing protectively over the vivid sparking, blinking sea.

Today
I stood on a slug
In my socks
In the rain
Picking wet clothes up from the mud
And looked across the dirty houses
To a sea of manure coloured sludge

Yesterday
Stunned by the colours of the garden's flowers
I came inside to see the glee on my daughter's face as she ran
Joyfully gurgling through the expanse of this lovely house.

Today
I sat
Forever
Cleaning her vomit from the oatmeal shag pile
Of this lovely house
Which is not ours
And on which we can't afford the rent

Yesterday
Playing football with my son
I caught a glimpse, a glance of something on his face
From a long ago photograph of me playing on a beach

With my dad
With joy
And I thought
'God, he's just like me'

Today
Playing football with my son
In the house like we've been told not to
I saw him go to take a free kick
And, running up
Trip over the rug and smash his head on the door
And I thought
'Oh God, he's just like me'

Yesterday
Beer in hand
I screamed and cheered with the red half of the pub
As this year's genius announced himself with
Touch
Vision
And Power

Today
Aspirin in hand
I looked at the paper
And read a figure
Sixty thousand pounds a week
Above a picture of a potato-faced kid
Who is eighteen.

Yesterday
I was thirty-nine

Today
I am

Not

*Mike Counsell*

# At the Café Moon

A scrap of silver paper abandoned on a plate,
Idly I finger fashion it into shapes,
and there you are before me again
in your butterfly form, just as you came
to me on the night I learned of your death,
at ease on the wall beside my head.

It saddens me that I cannot find
the whole of your face at once, the lined
cheeks, yes, the boxer's chin behind
the curtain of beard, those sailor blue eyes,
doubtful lips. But these will not suffice
for I want it all.

As time goes on,
more and more bits of you will be gone
till all that remains is a haunting, remembered perfume
or the half-lost echo of a beloved tune.

*Mary Rothwell*

# In Search of Andrew Young

It was a windy day in late March. There had been heavy rain overnight, and there was still rain in the wind. It was the day I had set aside for a visit to the church at Stonegate.

I left Stonegate station and my way was lined by the parked cars of commuters. There was still rain in the wind. I came out onto a main road and was splashed by a car. I looked up the road. Where was Stonegate? I set off uphill in hope. Wind threw rain against my cheek.

It was a long road with curves. Sometimes the verge was a mere ledge or perch, sometimes not even that.

Stonegate, where was Stonegate?

I zigzagged for reasons of safety. Did a curve hide a coming car? And I'd stand with my back to the road as a car splurged by.

There was something squashed on the road. I thought it might be a squirrel, then I saw its beak. The bird was the grey colour of the road, but the thick gouts of blood by its side were bright as berries.

Again I came upon a shy huddled group of pale yellow wayside flowers. This time I counted the petals: five. The flowers had orange centres. Were they primroses? Andrew Young would have known. And have given a name to those sparse withered berries that hung above a bleached wooded railing that branches were helping to prop.

I paused by a gate and looked at the mud on the brow of a field. There were two pools in the mud. One was olive-green and the other was sky-grey. Both of the pools were still, then the grey one shuddered.

I had come to purpose-made pathway. I saw ahead was it the roof of a bus-stop shelter? Buses? No, it was the broach-spire roof of a lychgate. I had arrived: here was Saint Peter's Church, Stonegate, where once Andrew Young was vicar. A pollard tree in the grounds had bristling dark knurrs and fresh-looking amputations.

Was the church door just hard to open? No, it was well and truly locked. I looked about in the grounds, but half-heartedly. After all, Andrew Young had come from elsewhere, spent eighteen years here, then on his retirement had gone elsewhere. I could see no plaque to him.

I met not a soul about.

I stood again in the grounds of the church. The clock was at a standstill, though the minute rod sometimes trembled. So too did the grass. Daffodils I did know by name. They were standing in seasonal resurrection, if curved by the wind. I thought of that poem by Andrew Young in which as a ghostly presence he witnesses a burial in those very grounds, then it dawns on him it's his own.

I gave up the ghost of my quest. I set off back to the station with rain on the other cheek. I counted petals on the way.

In the waiting room a white-haired man was leaning on his stick as he bent over a bench. He was tidying with one hand and with houseproud care two piles of freebies, the Wealden. Did he, I asked him, live locally?

He straightened and looked at me. His face was pale and clear, his eyes were bright and dark, perhaps like those withered berries had once been. My face still felt wet. 'Yes I do,' he said. '*Very* locally.' He cocked his thumb to the wall. 'Next-door as a matter of fact. I'm the station master. Twice retired.'

'Have you lived in these parts long then?''

'Oh yes. A very long time.' He took two papers from one pile and put them on the other.

'I wonder,' I said. 'I've been to the church but it's locked. Did you know Andrew Young I wonder? He used to be vicar there. I only know him for his poetry.'

'Oh yes, I knew Andrew Young. I knew him in a manner of speaking, and that's perhaps as much as most people could say, they knew him in a manner of speaking. He was a shy man is the way I would put it. But not so shy in his sermons, to go mostly by what I was told. Not so shy on the matter of death. I won't be gone a minute.'

He had left his stick on the bench, as a bridge supported by the two piles of papers. The handle of the stick was a question mark.

'The church,' he said, coming back from the platform. 'The church would have been locked because of vandals.'

'Vandals? Vandals in Stonegate?'

'Well, I don't know where they come from.' His pale smooth skin and white hair made his eyes very dark and bright. He cocked his thumb at the other wall. 'It's the same with the toilets out here. That's why *they're* locked.

- 86 -

But if you *had* gone into the church and turned left it is, you'd have seen a plaque to Andrew Young. I can see it now on the wall, though it's a while since I've been there, quite a while. Marble, I'm almost sure. A marble plaque. To Andrew Young. Let me tell you this now. He'd come to my house on one of his visits and sit there and not say a word to me. Nor would I to him. We'd sit there like we're sitting here except there wouldn't be a word between us. Not that I'd feel uncomfortable, I'll say that, he never made me feel uncomfortable. Or impatient, for all that I do like to he doing. We'd sit there in silence and before you knew it we'd be sitting in the dark. By and by he'd be on his way, and I'm on *my* feet now, as I'm sure that's your train coming.'

I followed him onto the platform. My journey had not been fruitless.

**Kenneth Overend**

# Goodbye

Suddenly it hit me, as clear as day. I was making a terrible mistake and my stomach melted to churning water.

'Please stop,' I begged, anxiously tapping the taxi driver on the shoulder. 'I have to go back. Quickly. Please.'

'Whatever you say lady,' grumbled the driver, and his head hunched even lower.

Please God let me get there before he finds the note. I could still see it propped against the blue and white striped jug on the kitchen table. How could I have been so stupid?

Okay, Jim's never been the best lover in the world; but then, perhaps I haven't either. It's a fact men do slow down when they pass fifty; but, if I'm honest, I lost interest as soon as we'd had the kids. Now they've left home and Jim's sole interest is his beloved chickens. Maybe if I'd been a Rhode Island Red?

The taxi turned up Rosemont Avenue.

If only I hadn't felt so left out, surplus, unwanted.

Suppose I was ripe for it when Jim suggested I should get an outside interest. So I did. And at first Family History was fascinating, almost addictive. Then I met Damien ... Now, he *is* addictive.

We turned into Wooded Way and absently I noticed that the rowan trees were breaking into leaf.

How could I have ever thought of leaving...?

I pushed up my cuff and gasped. Twenty to eight! Oh come on!

I tried to calm my racing heart by breathing deeply. There's still time; usually Jim didn't appear on Sundays till gone eight-thirty, all puffy-eyed and still half-asleep.

Perhaps *that's* where it all went wrong: separate bedrooms!

I should've tried harder. But I'll make it up...

'Here we are, lady. High Briars? Okay?'

I grabbed my holdall.

'That'll be –'

I didn't wait, just pushed a crumpled ten-pound note into his hand and ran up the front path, the bloody holdall protesting against my leg. Everything became clumsy. I pulled my clutch bag open and yanked out my keys, spewing make-up and money onto the pathway.

Finally, I fumbled the key into the lock, turned it and pushed open the door.

Silence!

My note was still there and gratefully I stuffed it in my pocket. I stealthily crept into my room, pulled the door to, then slowly lowered myself onto the edge of the bed.

Sweat streamed down my face.

I'll undress and get back into bed. I'll phone Damien later; then, when I've calmed down a bit, I'll get up as normal.

I jerked with shock as the phone on my bedside cabinet suddenly jangled. I grabbed it and was stunned to hear Jim's voice on his extension.

'She's gone, Damien, come on round. Yes, she left a note; it's still on the kitchen table. We're free!'

*John Vallender*

# Morality

Not popular with the younger generation
The rules of life need some explanation,
How easy are the pitfalls before us
Quite soon they seem to be laborious.

Youth with its ever ready zest
Can lead astray the very best,
So many bright ideas over the years
End in heartache, suffering and tears.

Writers and moralists will view
The ever adventurous striving few,
Keeping on the straight and narrow
Could be their aspiration, not sorrow.

How many heartaches will occur
Because of selfish aims that appear?
Better a simple lifestyle gain,
Than all those years just lived in vain.

*Bill Burkitt*

# The Last Train

In the grey of a London day:
My passage home was not planned to stay.
As I look to days of the past: A happiness that was not meant to last.
And as I open up that door: I remember a lady of the past.

In the haze of a London that glowed
A wealth of happiness that overflowed
We gathered on that hot summer's day, in Hyde Park.
The Rolling Stones in concert: They set free butterflies
that soared like the lark.

In my inner mind I was clear.
That my ticket I held there was no fear.
My trip to return home was planned, a ticket clutched tightly
within my hand.
In the post train, my memories expand.

I remember 'Straw Dogs' too, from this time.
Memory drifts through fore time.
And as I reflect, I hear a heartbeat pounding through:
The tracks: compound this love in review.

Now in the darkness of the day,
A new happiness has come my way:
I know my home is cosy and warm,
The 'Last Train' transports me to that inner calm.

*Ann Hubbard*

# Lollipop

Des heaved another side of pork onto the wooden chopping board in the family shop. He'd worked here since leaving school; his dad and uncle had taught him. Now in his mid-thirties the cleaver was his tool, his medieval weapon. He slashed down, expertly dividing with a resounding chomp.

'That'll be £1.45 missus,' his voice rising to Eve the cashier, 'and the old man will be more than grateful.' He winked at a jolly red-faced 50-year-old Mrs Hewitt.

Eve grinned. She adored him and had done ever since she started there six years ago. It was his arms mostly, an extension of the cleaver, honed by natural effort and rising up to shoulders bursting out of his t-shirt.

Des had grown into a cheeky bugger. He had watched his father and uncle cajole those women to an extra few ounces on every deal.

'Go on missus, have that other sausage, I bet you haven't seen a beauty like that for a long time.'

He used to blush in his teens when some of the factory girls taunted him but now he reckoned he knew and understood women a whole lot more. He and Eve had been going out for two years and he knew matrimony was imminent. He didn't fight it, Eve was pretty and intelligent and a bit more than willing, as she responded to any snatched opportunity to slake their lust.

Eve laughed as she watched yet another woman suffering his wit. A slightly built nervous blonde held her hand out as he slapped some pork chops in while holding the hand underneath with his other hand, 'Bit of kidney in there'll put hairs on your chest'. Eve didn't hear the giggled retort as the youngster blushed, then as she took her money she recognised young Kim from the social club.

'Hello Kim, how's your Trevor? Is he still away? Still won't be long now eh?'

On reflection that had been the start of her suspicions. Des added to them with his feeble reasons for the dog walking, which had turned into four-hour long marathons with the dog looking fresh as a daisy and his after-shaved self dropping into the armchair and dozing off for the rest of their evenings at Eve's flat.

Eve's dream of married bliss with her testosterone hunk started to diminish with each refusal to name a date and make plans. Kim was quite a regular now, not big amounts but Eve wondered if she was on the Atkins diet.

Weeks later another day in the shop found Eve daydreaming, trying to see the future, when a thump, thump, thump brought her round. Uncle Ken went over to the freezer room sighing and tutting as he opened up, letting Des out with a 'How many times have I told you to get that lock looked at?'

'Its OK Unc, I'll get my tools tomorrow and soon fix it'.

Kim joined the queue and just glancing up from the till Eve could swear she saw a mouthed 'Hello' from Des. Her heartbeat quickened 'He is isn't he?' she wanted to scream, tears threatened, she bit her lip. The rest of the day she took money like an automaton.

That night at her place she let go.

'Are you seeing someone else, Des?'

'No, don't be silly darling' but his down turned eyes and foot shifting said the opposite.

'It's that little blonde tart isn't it? That ugly snub-nosed anorexic slut!'

His instinctive lying defence gave way as his feelings for Kim took over, making him leap stupidly to her defence like some lovelorn knight with a broken lance.

The shattering row that ensued left both of them drained; she fell sobbing into bed, their bed! Her torrent of tears matched the rain that fell on Des as he slunk away down the dark drizzling alley.

Life carries on though and she needed the steady income from the job.

'So get a life,' she told her reflection, 'put on a face and some lippy and best foot forward.'

It was strained at first, the banter went, that warm smile for her becoming an actor's grin for the customers. She never lost it though, that singular feeling of Des being the only one to give her life purpose, until that chance day when she saw him arm in arm in the park with Kim; then the wound turned septic and she seethed.

Her revenge was not vindictive though; she would make him realise what he was missing. She started keep fit, her good figure getting better, and her breasts firming and lifting. Good clothes too, revealing clothes, she knew his chinks and his weaknesses. Des couldn't help a crafty look at her cleavage in the pay kiosk. Well, well, she wondered, could there still be something or would he even cheat on Kim just for gratification?

In the early days they had grabbed heated moments in the freezer room, the smell of the meat had seemed to turn him on and she didn't mind being rammed against a side of beef.

At the end of a busy Friday they were alone. Des was checking stock, Eve had slipped out of her overalls and stood in the freezer doorway, her see-through skirt silhouetted beautifully. She watched as he smiled that old smile. She went in, hanging her arms around his neck and kissing deep and long. 'Just a minute, I'll turn the closed sign around'.

Eve slipped away out to the shop door briefly touching the inner handle, still not properly fixed. She looked back at Des cockily grinning, grasping a hanging hook.

She turned away, looking only forward, and the door closed softly behind her.

*John Stevens*

# Happy Birthday

Mark Chapman glances, no not Mark Chapman, that's the same name as the bloke who shot Lennon. Martin something? Campbell? Never liked the name Campbell. It'll have to do.

Martin Campbell puts down his beer, managing to avoid spilling any this time, and glances around the room. You can't really describe parties as going full swing these days. The party was going at about half to two-thirds of a swing, which is about as good as it gets for a room full of thirty-five to forty-five year olds, especially when most have got nought to twelve-year-olds somewhere on the premises, asleep or playing PS2, or spying on the adults, the better to make blackmail notes in the morning.

This was a warm friendly middle-class house full of warm friendly middle-class people, most of whom Martin doesn't know, but a few he has known for a long time. There's Sally with Patrick, giggling behind their wine glasses. Martin looks across the room at the couple they're trying not to look as though they're looking at. A tall, ridiculously skinny man, who Martin was introduced to all of half an hour ago and now can't remember whether he's a vet or a quality control clerk, is taking advantage of the fact that his wife has left the room to try and chat up the nurse, or was she a teacher? She is having nothing of it.

This is as scandalous as the night will get. Martin will not end the evening sat outside with Sally, wallowing in self-pity and comparing notes as to whose life most closely resembles The Smiths' 'I know it's over.' Kimmy will not drink to the extent that she loses control of her legs and call pathetically, 'I want Tom, I want Tom,' for hours on end as she did at a party twenty-odd years ago, to the extent that the phrase was called at her by everybody who knew her for weeks after the party, every time she entered a room. Martin smiles to himself and wanders into the next room, where Tom is playing Elton John songs at the piano while a red wine bottle sits close by. Twenty years ago he'd have been, well, to be fair to him he'd have been sat by a red wine bottle and plunking out Elton John songs. Actually any social gathering involving alcohol and a piano for the last couple of decades has seen Tom banging out *Your Song*. His brother Sam is trying to remember the words to *Daniel* while simultaneously conversing with a college lecturer they've just met about some new literary book Martin has heard of but not read. His wife Delia is smiling indulgently at him.

'Don't you just love it when he gets pompous?'

Martin smiles and looks around the room. There are photographs, framed photographs, tastefully and artfully arranged on most of the walls, and Martin remembers other photographs on other walls. University walls would have a collage of them over a bed or pinned to a peeling cork message board. Martin had millions of photographs at one point, in his dingiest bedsit, as a cheap alternative to wallpaper. The difference was that the walls of Tom and Kimmy's house didn't have any pictures of anyone lying on a bathroom floor, naked with freshly shorn eyebrows, or throwing up over a television. Tom invites Martin to sing with his eyes, and …

'How can you sing with your eyes?' Mike looked around. Jo was handing him a cup of tea and reading over his shoulder.

'That's not what it means.'

'Didn't think so. Reads like that though.'

'Yeah, I'll re-write that bit. I might re-write the whole thing actually.'

'Not going well?' she asked as she sat down.

'No.' He ran his hands through his hair. 'The problem is I don't know what I'm doing.'

'I can see how that might be a problem.'

'I just thought I'd do this thing about the nature of friendship, long term friendship, and tie it into our fortieth birthdays, and I can't quite see how to get it to work.'

Jo stood up, kissed him on the forehead and said, ' You'll be all right. I'm sure you'll think of something.' She closed the door behind her and he could hear her limping down the stairs, breaking in her new shoes.

'Oh well, that's all right then,' muttered Mike under his breath. 'As long as you're sure I'll think of something. Big help you are.' He printed off what he'd already written, read it and shook his head. He leant back, rubbed his eyes, pushed back his chair and said 'Bed time.' He carried his tea and his stack of paper downstairs to the kitchen to see Jo bent over her laptop and rubbing at her own eyes. 'You okay?' he said, putting down his tea and starting to knead her shoulders.

'It's this report. I know what I want to say but I'm struggling to tie in the recommendations to the actual information from each school.'

'Let's have a look then.' He pulled up a chair next to hers and started reading. 'I wouldn't do it in this order. If you shift all your results up here it'd be easier for you to...'

She turned the screen back toward her. 'If it's all right with you I think I'll do it my own way.'

Mike was suddenly angry. 'I'm trying to help,' he shouted.

'Well you're not helping, you're patronising. I think I know a little more about education than you do. And when I need your help I'll ask for it.'

'You did ask for it.' Mike's voice was now rising to the point where he knew it sounded silly and squeaky; it always did when he was fiercely arguing on a point of principle.

'I didn't, and stop shouting.'

'You did, and I'm not shouting,' he shouted.

'I said I was having one or two problems with it. I do not need your help.'

'Well what's the point of telling me then? What's the point of telling anybody unless you think they can help?

'Do you have to be such a typical man? Ninety-nine times out of a hundred if I tell you my problems it's because I want a bit of sympathy. A bit of understanding. Trust me; I do not want your help with my job.'

Mike's anger sank away as quickly as it had risen. 'So presumably that's why, when I ask for your help, I get a 'there, there,' and a pat on the head, rather than anything constructive.'

'You actually wanted my help?' Jo looked surprised. 'Pass it over then. What are you trying to do? '

'That's what I've written so far, and there are some notes here. Well, the idea was to try and do some kind of fictional account of a party, and compare it with memories of teenage parties with the same people.' He pushed his fingers together. It was something he'd started to do years ago to make him look thoughtful and clever. Now it was a habit he hated catching himself doing. It usually meant he was being self-important. 'To show how we've changed and how we haven't, and try to capture something of the nature, the importance of this friendsh...what?'

Jo was giggling. 'Tom and Kimmy Froth?'

'Not necessarily.'

'What's Sally and Patrick's surname?'

'I'm not saying. If all you can do is snigger I think I might reconsider asking for your advice.'

'Is it MacAlpine?' Jo's laughter was getting close to out of control now. Mike was trying to hang on to his dignity.

'I think it's best if I just work on it myself. '

'No, no,' said Jo bringing herself under control. 'I'll be good.'

'Right then. It's MacTaggart, at the moment. Although I could change it. I suppose I'd better warn you that you're about to come across Sam and Delia as well.'

That was sufficient. Jo was curling up repeating the word Delia to herself under her struggling breath.

'Oh for God's sake,' said Mike and stalked out of the room. He looked out of the back window. He had forgotten to bring the clothes in. He unlocked the back door and let himself out. The night was clear, and there was a strong breeze blowing up the hill. The air smelt of the sea. When they'd first moved down it was really strong, but it was only occasionally now that he noticed. In 1970s Warrington it had been the stale beer smell of the brewery that was strong enough to get used to. The brewery was gone now.

He picked the clothes, damp with dew, from the line and made his way back in to the house. He locked the back door and went to check the front.

Jo was still reading, and no longer laughing. 'So what's the problem, names apart?'

'It's supposed to be fictional. Which means there should be a story, but I don't want … things happening.'

'Well, that's okay, you could just do it as an observation, as a slice of life piece, but you'd need more about the actual people.'

'I've never liked those. And I'm not going to write about real people. It's not like when they're your own characters. You can only get them wrong.'

'Well, make up the characters then. Do something about the concept of friendship.'

'Not specific enough.'

'So. To sum up. You want to do this kind of big thank you stroke happy birthday thing. You want to do it fictionally, with no story. You want to be specific, with recognisable people, but you want to write nothing specific about them, and you want to do it with ludicrous names.'

'These are people to whom I owe a lot. My sanity, my belief in the redemptive possibilities of humanity, copious amounts of money.'

'Have you considered birthday cards? You could write "Thank you for your friendship" inside.'

'I should just forget it, shouldn't I?'

'Your call.'

'Yeah.'

'Is the front door locked?'

'I'm just going to check it now.'

'See you upstairs.'

'Yeah. And thanks, Jo.'

Jo went upstairs, and he could hear her brushing her teeth as he locked the front door and turned the lights off.

It is the following evening. Tom and Martin are sat at the table.

'Chinese?' says Tom

'Depends,' says Martin, 'I'm a bit fussy about my Chinese.'

'It's a really good one,' says Kimmy as she comes into the room, 'I don't mind cooking though, there's stuff in the fridge.'

'You've done enough,' says Sally, 'and besides I'd have to offer to help and I'm not going to.'

'I much prefer crap Chinese to good ones,' says Martin. ' When I order chicken chow mein I want to know that I'm getting grey slabs of possible chicken lying on noodles. Last week I got one and it had vegetables in it, and some sort of proper sauce.'

'I know what you mean,' says Sally, 'I always think you can judge a Chinese by its sweet and sour pork. If the sauce doesn't look like it contains radioactive fallout I'm not interested.'

'And the pork balls should be about eighty-five percent fat.'

Tom orders the special banquet.

'You don't want MSG do you?' he asks Martin, his hand over the phone.

'MSG?'

'Monosodium glutamate. It's a flavour enhancer, but they'll leave it off if you ask them.'

'Why would you ask them to leave off something that enhances the flavour?'

'It's not good for you,' says Kimmy as she searches under the cushions for the phone.

'That settles it then.'

'You're incorrigible.'

'Of course in my head it still stands for the Michael Schenker Group,' Tom laughs.

When he finished in the bathroom she was already in bed, doing the crossword.

'Araucaria alphabetical!' she said with a smile.

'What? Oh the crossword.' He put his light on.

'The other thing you could do,' she said, turning to him, 'is to write about how difficult it is to write what you're trying to, to come back a level and have somebody comment on it. You could do that as fiction.'

'No I hate all that. All that tricksy stuff. Writing about writing. Drawing attention to the fiction, breaking the fourth wall, all that stuff. Is that meta-fiction? Or is that something else?'

'Don't know.'

'Neither do I. Doesn't matter. I'm not doing it.'

There were a few minutes of near silence, only interrupted by Jo's pen scribbling notes around the margin of the crossword.

'Are you going to be long with the crossword?'

'Don't have to be.'

'No it's okay. I'll try and do a bit more.'

It is two hours later. They have got through three quarters of a Chinese banquet and several bottles of European lager. Tom's eyes are twitching towards the piano. Sally is looking through their CDs.

'Have you got anything that's not crap?' she laughs.

'Piss off. Just 'cause I've got nothing that says "look at me I'm trying to be sixteen." '

'You don't have to pretend to be sixty though. Elton John, Elton John, Elton John, Randy Newman, did you pick that one up by mistake? Elton John, Lloyd-Webber. Busted's the best thing on this shelf.'

Martin and Kimmy are looking at the photographs on the wall again.

'Are there any of the four of us?'

'Yes actually, I was looking at the France ones the other day.' Martin settles himself down to the joyful horror at looking at them all in adolescence.

'That's not fair. You all look better now.'

'That can't be true,' says Kimmy. 'Oh my God look at me there. I hope I do look better now.'

'It's not just that one, you're much more… sorted looking now. Here you look…'

'Gormless?' This is Tom

'You can talk, look at you,' she says, waving a photo under his nose.

'I was probably ill. Who's that bloke next to me?'

'I do believe that's me.' says Sally. 'And the girl on the other side…'

'Is me,' says Martin. And that's how they spend the rest of the evening. Laughing, drinking and pointing at embarrassing pictures.

'I tried to get a bit of conflict going in there by having an internal debate about moving into the middle class. It comes across like I'm criticizing their taste in photographs.'

'Why? You're all middle class.'

'Matter of opinion.'

'What's the point in trying to add conflict when you're talking about friendship?'

'Fiction is conflict.'

'Yes, but it's not going to get across what you're after is it? If you're going to be close to someone for years you're not going to be arguing all the time are you?'

'Suppose not. Fancy a cuddle?'

'Early start tomorrow.'

'Okay.' He snaked his way around her body to his favourite feeling of contented safety. 'Love you.'

She stroked his hair.

'Love you too.'

*Mike Counsell*

# The Empty Canvas

The empty canvas
Leans against the wall
Patiently waiting
Tubes of paint
Parade before my eyes
Hungrily gathered
Cascades of colour explode
Where to begin
The paint brush trembles
Between my fingers
Slowly the dance begins
Swathes of colour
Twist and twirl
Images emerge
Spaces become places
Skies, seas, mountains and trees
Time to pause
Catch my breath
Go back
Come forward
Take out
Put in

Finally
The dance ends
In the stillness
The paint dries
Not yet complete
Select a frame
Find a place
That has a space
Where the light of day
Illuminates the shadows
Is the hanging
    Completion
Or another beginning?

**Linda Mooncie**

# Bargain Christmas

Churches are empty
Supermarkets full
Bells silent
Cash registers ringing
Processions of worshippers
Processions of purchasers
Between the aisles
Three kings bearing gifts
Buy two get one free
Shepherds tending flocks
Managers checking stocks
Christmas cards
Credit cards
Where is the child
The stable bare
Lost to mankind
Amongst the fayre.

***Linda Mooncie***

# Childhood

I recall
Innocent pleasures
Gathering rose petals
When no one was watching
To put in a jam jar
Pour in the water
Hide in the garden
Expecting wonderful perfume
As the days passed by
Promises of perfume faded
As the petals decayed.

I recall
Innocent pleasures
Picking the privet hedge
Removing the leaves
Making a circle
Collecting dew laden early morning cobwebs
Weaving fairy handkerchiefs
Somehow the lace becomes grey
As the days passed by
Promises of fairy visits faded
As the cobwebs decayed.

*Linda Mooncie*

# Vintage Beauties

There I was, in a high-rise council flat in Hollington by the sea, mother of four. Kerry, thirteen, stays up till 11pm; Sean, ten and a half, goes to the ramp park with his friends after school to show off his skills with the mountain bike uncle Jack happened to find in the back of an abandoned lorry. Lisa, who's six, drives me Barbie mad and Timothy, who is three, is still in the throes of his 'terrible twos'. Their dad left when I fell pregnant with Timothy. We agreed on just two kids, but the other two sort of popped out as fate dictated.

Well, thirteen years since my first pregnancy ended and a lot of comfort eating and bickie-breaks later, I'm pretty voluptuous, as I like to think of myself. I've still got a waist, well sort of, my thighs have ballooned, my buttocks expanded, my boobs have bloomed and my arms and tummy have a healthy covering of insulating puppy fat. Okay, I'm fat! Well so what, get over it, most of us Brits are overweight, so join the club. It doesn't help that I drive everywhere either.

My story begins when for the first time I got a real break from motherhood; Timothy went to nursery full time. That's two and a half hours a day, five days a week in real terms; the blasted council wouldn't pay for any more. In London, parents get tokens from 8am to 6pm, so their job centres can tell them to get back out to work, something I've longed to do. There's only so much child time you can have a week and then you need some decent adult company: I mean girlfriends, boyfriends, just platonic, you know, but adult talk, no curfew rules.

Our parents used to kick us out on the street to play, 'Just be back in time for tea.' Do you remember? No such luck nowadays; motherhood's a prison sentence, or so it seemed until that late April afternoon, when I dropped Timothy off at the Hippo club and walked down with Tash and Beckie to the beach opposite the pavilion.

It was closed that day, so we went back up to street level and bought some bubbly (Lambrini, not the real stuff), a whole five-litre giant size bottle. We were so busy talking about exes and what we'd have done if we'd never met them or got pregnant, we got a little carried away with drinking ourselves into the realms of fantasy land. None of us had much time for drinking now (what with the kids 'n' all), so we got tiddly quicker I suppose. Anyhow, there we was, saying how we'd have done the catwalk in glitzy south of France, lowering our cardigans and prancing about on the pebbles, (nearly killing ourselves in our 'Next' high-heeled shoes), and falling over in peals of tiddly laughter, when Beckie pulls out this camera and starts clicking. Well, we all jumped at the chance of being caught on camera in our sexiest positions (dressed of course) each of us snatching the camera and snapping the other two making complete fools of themselves. The film didn't last long; all thirty-six exposures were used up in a matter of minutes. Then we went to a café, and had some coffee to try and sober up before collecting the kids!

The next day we all agreed to destroy the film, but Beckie, silly cow, had reloaded the camera, and put the used film in with the other undeveloped ones of her and her brood on holiday, and forgotten which one was which, cause they all looked the bloody same. Well, they would wouldn't they? She'd bought them from Lidl, four in a pack for a fiver, special offer. That's Beckie for you, head in the clouds as usual. We agreed to send them all off to a photographic lab up north, you know one of those packet things, that come in with the junk mail, so no one who knew us would see them. I was terrified; post was going missing all the time, what if one of the posties who knew us opened the damn thing?

It was May 16th when Beckie phoned me, eight bloody thirty in the morning, school run for me. All right for Becky, both of hers take themselves to secondary school and have each other for safety and all.

I remember her screeching down the phone, 'The photos have come! Get over here! You've got to see them, they're bleeding amazing!'

Kerry always went to school early to meet up with her mates, but I still had to drive Sean and Lisa to St. Paul's for 8.50 am and take a buggy and bag of nibbles and bits for Timothy. Tim wet every now and again if we didn't make it to a toilet in time, so a few extra sets of clothes were in order. I rushed all the way to Becky's and still arrived after Tash. We put CBBIES on for Timothy, and huddled on Becky's sofa to see the photos. Beckie was clasping the closed packet, keeping us in suspense; Tash and I went to snatch them. 'Now, now,' said Beckie, holding them up high. 'All in good time,' she said, as she slowly opened the packet, pulling them out like they was valuables.

We looked at the photos alright. I remember thinking 'Wow! Is that really me?' For so many years I'd stood in front of mirrors thinking, 'Fat cow' and to look at me there in those photos, I might be a big girl, but Christ, I am still young and beautiful! Everything in its place, slightly exaggerated proportions admittedly, but still sexy.

It all kicked off from there really. Beckie was awaiting her City and Guilds diploma in photography, Tash had done a business start up course via the benefits agency, and I came up with the alternative modelling agency, called 'Vintage Beauties'.

We started off by making our own calendar and advertising in the Friday Ad for 'Voluptuous oversized models, no experience necessary!' We even got a grant from the Hastings Trust and patented our idea. Now we've had national exposure via the News and put Hastings back on the map for creativity, imaginative ingenuity and modelling with a difference. Voluptuous women are most definitely back in fashion!

By the way, that picture of me has only ended up on the cover of *The Lady* Magazine. Oh, and I almost forgot, I'm buying my own home with a garden in West St. Leonards: very posh!

I get to have a laugh, get tiddly, get my kit off and get paid for it! Who said you can't have your cake and eat it!

*Tania Oriol*

# Read On...

'If my kids are off school sick I can't even write a note to their teacher to explain,' says Jenny, in her twenties with two young children. 'And my husband has to read out the directions on their medicine bottles.'

It's really hard to imagine what life would be like if, like Jenny, you couldn't read or write. Try thinking about it for a moment. It means far more than not being able to enjoy the pleasures of a good book, or to write whatever you want. It can mean all sorts of problems in everyday life. Words that most of us need to glance at only briefly to understand can mean nothing at all to some people.

Jenny badly wants to be able to help her children with their school work and read books with them. She says, 'I want to be involved. Be a good mother. I don't want them to think I'm thick or be ashamed of me.'

Being thought of as stupid, or backward, is a common experience for those without basic literacy skills. Jenny remembers being ridiculed as a child in front of the whole class when she couldn't grasp something. The humiliation struck deep and left her in tears. 'I hated school after that and didn't learn much,' she explains, 'I bunked off as much as I could and played around the rest. Nobody really cared. I didn't realise then how important reading and writing are.'

Jenny is far from stupid. She's a sociable person, involved in lots of things. She can take part in intelligent discussions and give her opinions. She is good at arts and crafts. She's a capable and caring mother. She just hasn't developed her reading and writing skills.

Jenny is not alone. Many thousands of people leave school with barely basic literacy skills. Take Paul, who works in a garage. He's a competent mechanic who has no problem fixing cars. It's something he loves doing. But ask him to fill in a work-sheet and he can't manage. Someone has to complete it for him. Not being able to do the paperwork in his job means his prospects are limited. It's holding him back and keeping his earnings low.

Elaine always relied heavily on her husband's support to cover her lack of literacy skills. Now divorced and alone, she is worried when the post arrives. 'I don't know what's important and what isn't. Forms frighten me so I usually throw them away. Once there was a notice put in the door to say the water was going to be cut off - I couldn't read it so I just ignored it. I was in the middle of washing my hair when, suddenly, no more water came out of the tap! Sometimes I ask someone to read things to me, but it's embarrassing.'

These are just a few examples of the difficulties experienced by those who find reading a problem. It's often seen as somehow shameful to admit in public you can't read and many become adept at covering it up. All sorts of excuses or ploys are made to avoid possible embarrassment. A favourite is: 'Sorry – I can't see to fill this in. I've left my glasses behind.' Or, 'I'll have the same as you,' for those unable to read a restaurant menu.

Therefore it's a very positive step when people do what Jenny, Paul and Elaine have done and sign up for Adult Basic Literacy classes.

'I was very nervous of going - in fact petrified - and nearly didn't! But it's OK. Nobody laughs at me. We work in a small group and we're all in the same boat,' explained Jenny.

Paul likes the way students can work on what is relevant to them. 'I've actually brought in the worksheets I need for my job. And I'm learning to read and write the words I need to use most often.'

This is the way these students learn. Not with inappropriate children's books such as *Janet and John*, which were sometimes used in the past for adults, but with material of interest and relevance to each individual.

The class tutor explained, 'We often use what is called the "language experience" approach. This means the reading material used is devised from the students' own words and experiences, listened to and written down by the tutor. Students then start by learning to read, write and spell the most familiar words they use when speaking. It works well and they build up from there.'

The key to learning is a friendly, supportive and relaxed atmosphere. Classes are always kept small and informal. Nobody needs to be embarrassed, even if they can't write their own name. They are all there for the same reason – they have some problem with reading and writing and they want to improve.

'Usually there are not more than six students, so they can all benefit from some individual support. As well as group work, we also draw up personalised workplans at the beginning of each term. All students can choose what they want to concentrate on. It could be filling forms, writing letters, reading recipes, or even something as basic as learning the alphabet or being able to use a telephone directory. Everybody has something different they want to work on. The choice is theirs. We just help them on their chosen path.'

Helen, newly retired, is a volunteer Basic Education literacy tutor working alongside the paid tutor. Her help is invaluable, as it means more one-to-one tuition is available. 'The reason I do this work is because I enjoy reading so much myself. I couldn't imagine life without books! When I applied to do this voluntary work I thought I could just go along and lend a hand, but then I found that I had to be properly trained first.'

She explained that the training had involved ten sessions at college on Saturday mornings, completing six assignments and building up a portfolio, as well as being on placement in an Adult Literacy class. Although she initially found the work daunting, it was stimulating and enjoyable too.

'One early exercise we had to do was to keep a record, for one day, of every single thing we did that needed literacy skills. It wasn't just obvious things like dealing with the post and reading the newspaper but also, for example, finding something in Yellow Pages, reading a notice at the station, choosing a card with the right words inside, reading instructions on labels, looking up TV programmes and so on. Ordinary things you do without thinking about. Certainly it made me much more aware about how difficult life can be if you can't read.' The training also covered creating and encouraging positive attitudes to learning, overcoming barriers, understanding how we learn, simplifying text and analysing readability, planning teaching sessions and evaluating resources.

Halfway through the training Helen was put on placement in an Adult Literacy class, firstly to observe the teaching and then to participate in it, putting her training into practice.

'I worked with a particular student on a one to one basis. Then, for one assignment, I was assessed on planning, carrying out and evaluating a teaching session for her. It all went very well. The training involved a lot more work than I imagined, but without it I wouldn't have known where to start or been so aware of the problems encountered.'

On successful completion of the training course, Helen gained a City and Guilds Initial Certificate in Teaching Basic Skills, a qualification that would be useful if she wanted to be a paid tutor, or a good foundation if she wanted to train further.

'However, I'm happy as a volunteer and do one morning a week. I really love it and it's so rewarding to see the students gaining confidence as they develop their literacy skills,' she said.

Basic Education departments (often linked to local colleges of further education) are always pleased to hear from prospective volunteers and courses are usually run yearly. More efforts are now being made to attract people who need help to come to classes – for example crèches are being set up to make it easier for young mothers to attend, disabled access is planned, and sometimes there are 'drop-in sessions' where students can come and go when it suits them.

It is important that the public is aware that the problem of illiteracy exists and, even more importantly, what is currently on offer to help.

***Rosemary Bartholomew***

# The Prize

'Are you one of the prize-winners?'

Katie handed over her coat to the hotel's cloak-room attendant. 'No,' she hesitated, 'but as a member of the Writers' Group, I still like to be here.' She forced a smile.

'Well, there's always next year isn't there?' The girl's smile was sympathetic.

Katie felt irritated as she stood in front of a mirror and touched up her lipstick. Even cloakroom attendants were feeling sorry for her now. She wondered why she kept turning up at the Awards Ceremony when she never won anything.

As a regular member for nearly a decade, entering all of their annual competitions each year without even a runner-up prize, she felt a failure. So many rejections of her writing efforts did nothing for her morale.

Most members had won something at some time or other. Maybe I am a failure, she thought, as she combed her thick red hair and twisted it up again into the neat coil that gave her an appearance of elegance and efficiency. Successful, yes, as junior partner in a firm of local solicitors, but not as a writer.

Ever since she'd been chosen to read out her composition at a school assembly at the age of eight, she'd fancied herself as an author. She remembered that composition very clearly. *A Day in the Life of a Lost Umbrella* she'd called it and was highly praised for her vivid imagination. But that was twenty years ago, she reminded herself. No amount of vivid imagination had helped her since. It was just brains and not imagination that had got her a degree.

At the Group meetings they were all very kind about the entries she submitted, offering their constructive criticism. She'd tried, she really had, but she knew her manuscripts were about as scintillating as one of her conveyancing agreements.

'Katie, so glad you were able to come.' Timothy Harton, the elderly chairman of the group, pushed his way through the crowd, and handed her a glass of wine. 'You're looking lovely tonight,' he said. 'We'll be starting soon. Just time for you to down a couple of glasses.' He laughed, gave her a fatherly hug, and moved on. Katie drained the contents of her glass and helped herself to another. What was she doing here with all these writers? Shouldn't she just be content with her professional career?

After her third glass of wine she joined the latecomers at the back of the conference room. There was the usual rustle of excitement as Sebastian Conrad threaded his way to the raised dais to be warmly greeted by the chairman.

For the last few years, Sebastian Conrad had been presenting the prizes. Tall, debonair and internationally successful with his science fiction novels, he was popular and generous with his sponsorship.

'He's an absolute dish, isn't he?' Maisie Hardcastle nudged Katie in the ribs. 'He could edit my manuscripts any time he wished!' She giggled foolishly.

Katie felt Maisie entered the competitions because of Sebastian Conrad. To walk up to the dais with photographers at the ready, and have the literary world's most eligible bachelor, according to *Hello* magazine, smile into your eyes as he handed over the prize, well, that was possibly an added incentive.

As the ceremony got under way, Katie smiled and clapped as the prizes were awarded, but was already thinking about slipping away and calling a taxi to take her home. The chairman was making his final speech. She was barely listening.

' … and last but not least we award a small prize to one of our most popular members for her untiring efforts and constant support.'

'Go on, Katie, it's for you.' Maisie Hardcastle, still clutching her *Writer of the Year* cup, hissed in her ear.

'What...?' Katie surfaced from her daydream and realised that a sea of faces were turned in her direction. She staggered to her feet, her colour rising. Although it was probably well meant, she felt awful. No prize at all was better than one for being a failure.

Resisting the urge to turn and run, she began the long walk to the platform. Whether it was the heat of the room, too much wine, or her high heels that caused her to trip on reaching the steps, she never knew. There was a buzz of shocked voices. She lay dazed, eyes closed, her humiliation increasing. Within seconds she was lifted and carried effortlessly out of the room.

Placed gently in a chair in the bar, a stool under her legs, and a large brandy in her shaking hand, she stared apologetically at Sebastian Conrad.

'I'm so sorry,' she muttered. 'What a stupid thing to do.' She rubbed her ankle, avoiding looking at him.

'It could happen to anyone. Those damn steps are treacherous.' He sounded concerned. 'How are you feeling?'

'A bit shaky.' And a bit of a mess, she thought, as she realised her hair was escaping from its pins and falling around her shoulders. She tried to pat her hair into shape.

'Don't bother about your hair, it looks great to me. Drink your brandy and I'll take you home.'

Katie shot him a startled glance. 'No, please. I'll call a taxi. Besides,' she added, 'you should go back.'

'I don't really want to,' he interjected quickly and then smiled, his eyes dancing with humour. 'They'll all be busy attacking the buffet. I'll be glad to escape.'

'Really?'

'Yes, really.' He glanced towards the conference room and lowered his voice. 'It sometimes gets a bit too much, being attacked by doting fans on all sides.' He shrugged and grinned again. 'Sounds uncharitable, I know. I do owe everything to the people who buy my books, but at functions like this I sometimes feel as though they've bought me as well.'

Katie laughed. She was finding him fun to be with. Although recognising his attractions, she'd never paid much attention to him before, thinking that it was only a platform personality that captured his audience. Like a lot of very successful men, she'd supposed he would be slightly arrogant and too pleased with himself, but his natural charm and close proximity were causing unfamiliar sensations to ripple over her. He was looking at his watch.

'Katie, it is Katie, isn't it?' She nodded. 'How d'you feel about coming and having a spot of supper at that new place round the corner? That is, if your ankle feels better.'

Katie had completely forgotten about her ankle. She felt slightly light-headed. 'I'd love to,' she said, 'but,' she hesitated, 'I've never read any of your books ... I hate science fiction.' She drained her glass and looked across at him with an impish grin. 'Still want to take me?'

'More than ever.' He smiled. 'At least I won't have to talk shop.' Suddenly serious, his dark eyes met hers.

'I've wanted to meet you before, but never had the chance. You've always disappeared before I could free myself from the others, and when I came to your office, you were nowhere around.'

Katie felt her heart leap in a most peculiar fashion. 'You've been to my office?'

'I wanted a spot of advice on a legal matter, nothing important, but they took me to see some old guy in a pin-striped suit.' He looked away nervously and Katie realised that he was actually shy. 'To be honest, it was an excuse. I'd already asked Tim Harton where you worked.'

'Oh!'

'I was looking for you … hope you don't mind.'

Katie was saved from having to reply as the chairman himself appeared, a sausage roll in one hand and a small square package in the other.

'Katie, my dear girl, how are you feeling?'

'Much better, thank you.'

'We were all so upset when you fell, but Sebastian insisted we carry on without you both.' He beamed at the author, before turning back to Katie. 'This is your little gift. You mustn't forget it.'

'Thank you.' She looked at the package. Probably a '*How to Write*' book, she thought, but suddenly it didn't matter any more. Her vivid imagination was already tearing off into deliciously romantic territories, and she didn't see why she should stop it.

'Come on, Katie, let's get your coat.' Sebastian helped her from the chair, a protective arm around her shoulders. 'Goodnight, Tim,' he said to the chairman, 'sorry about the hasty departure.' Then, with a knowing smile, 'I'm sure you'll understand. Katie and I have things to talk about.'

Katie felt she could read the cloakroom attendant's thoughts as she collected her coat. 'So you did get a prize after all?' The girl eyed the brightly ribboned package.

Katie nodded and gave her a radiant smile. Without having written a word, she knew she had walked off with the biggest prize of all.

*As this story is based on persons known to members of the Writers' Group the author prefers to remain anonymous.*

***Anon***

# Sydney Little: Visionary or Villain?

Complaining about Hastings has recently become a national pastime. Some local residents have always grumbled about the town and its facilities. Of course, there are always loyal supporters of the town who spring to its defence. How many are aware that many of their complaints can be traced back to the work of one man, Sydney Little, the Borough Engineer for Hastings from 1926 to 1950?

This is not to suggest that Little is to be blamed for any decline in the fortunes of the town. On the contrary, there can be no doubt that his arrival marked a turning point in the development of Hastings. As with all visionaries, however, not all his schemes were an unqualified success.

There can be no doubt that Little was an extremely competent professional engineer. Born in Carlisle in 1885 where his father was the Borough Surveyor, Sydney was elected to chartered membership of the Institution of Civil Engineers at the early age of twenty-five. He had already made a considerable impact in the profession by the time he came to Hastings. A pioneer in Britain of the then new concept of reinforced concrete, it was to be in Hastings that he earned the nickname of 'The Concrete King'. The development of the promenade as part of the Hastings sea defences is testimony to this reputation.

When called for interview for the job, he chose to spend the previous day walking round the town to see what needed to be done. He is reputed to have given the councillors on the interview panel a list of projects he considered essential and told them that, if appointed, he would expect their support in carrying out these schemes. This forthright approach to bureaucratic interference was to become a hallmark of his period of office.

Before his appointment Little had been Borough Engineer in Ipswich where, in 1922, he married his wife Angela. Their only daughter, Jean, was born in 1926, the year he came to Hastings. A devoted family man, he was also a keen gardener and tennis player. However, he kept his private life very much to himself and scant details are on record.

At work it was a very different story. Initially in charge of about fifty staff, he insisted on interviewing each one personally. Expecting the same degree of dedication from them as he gave himself he had a reputation for strictness, which, although fair, did not make him universally popular. On one occasion, while passing an excavation in the road, he noticed the workmen were leaning on their shovels rather than digging. He sacked the whole gang on the spot for time wasting. Unfortunately they were not council employees but Gas Board workmen who responded in predictable manner. This story circulated amongst council employees with many a secret chuckle.

Little was a small man and his supporters coined the phrase that 'he was big in everything except name and stature'. Despite, or perhaps because of his diminutive size, he was a great achiever. Also he could be scathing about incompetence. His views on what he saw as unnecessary bureaucratic interference earned him many enemies. On one occasion he gave a public address to the townsfolk, outlining his plans for the future of Hastings. During the following question time his lack of patience showed when he referred to opponents of his schemes as 'ignorant critics'. Nevertheless, he achieved considerable support from politicians at both local and national levels, successfully lobbying Parliament for his more prestigious schemes.

Sydney Little was to make his mark on the town as no other Borough Engineer before or since. Amongst his major achievements was the development of the town's water supply, in particular the construction of Darwell reservoir. He also supervised improvements in the Hastings main drainage system. Southern Water owe a great deal to the foresight of the man who developed these original works.

One of Little's first aims after appointment was to reconstruct the town's road system. To achieve this he removed the old tram tracks, much beloved by nostalgic citizens. Some months before his appointment, three thousand of these same citizens had signed a petition asking for a ten mile an hour speed limit along the front. Predictably, Sydney Little totally ignored this petition. His reconstruction of the sea front road has, arguably, left Hastings with an unfortunate legacy, dividing the town from its beach. It should be remembered however that he was dealing with pre-war traffic flow. The underground car park along the sea front was a part of this road contract. Although much maligned today, in its time it was a pioneering scheme, amongst the first in Britain.

He was also responsible for many minor works such as the pier-head bathing pool, Falaise Hall, the Bowls Pavilion and, an uncharacteristic touch of whimsy, Bottle Alley. Or perhaps it was his responsibility for refuse disposal that prompted him to line the walls with discarded bottles.

From 1940 to 1944 Sydney Little was on loan to the Admiralty where he was employed on the design of the Mulberry Harbour, a scheme of vital importance to the D-day landings. Many of Britain's top ranking engineers were employed on this project and Little's experience of reinforced concrete and sea defence work was to prove invaluable.

On his return to war-torn Hastings, Little came up with his most ambitious scheme for re-building the town. Based on his previous experience with the underground car park, he announced a plan to turn Hastings into a 'double deck city'. He constructed and displayed a model of this scheme that would have transformed the town and overcome many of the problems we have today. Unfortunately, following his retirement in 1949 his scheme was rejected.

One year after his retirement he was invited to the official opening of the Darwell Reservoir and in 1960 was granted honorary freedom of the borough, just one year before his death in 1961.

So, was he a visionary or a villain? The recent derogatory articles in the press newspaper painted a bleak picture of Hastings. Whether the criticisms were justified or not, the town has reacted in a positive manner. The latest initiative of the Tourist Action Group to regenerate the town is exciting and worthy of support from all political wings of the Borough Council. I suspect Sydney Little would be whole-heartedly leading the way, albeit with some controversial ideas of his own.

*Michael Smith*

# For a Golfing Friend

I am the writer with the motionless pen
I am the pen that hesitates
Scratching my message
Scant inadequate words
Words lacking comfort
Where is the comfort the pen cannot bring
Mind numbing loss
Church stones that sing
I am the song that never compensates
Never seeing again
Self-conscious tears
I am the tears of all those who know
Our friend
Somehow still with us
When summer winds blow

*Ken Baker*

# This

A bird sang a simple tune
In the intricate tree behind me,
And I heard a bird responding
Somewhere, somewhere beyond.

I saw the quick beak
Of the bird in the intricate tree,
And a squirrel played a snatch
On a peanut-shell harmonica.

It was only, only some days since,
This, and now I am grateful
I have found it where it was buried
And shelling it I can taste.

*Kenneth Overend*

# Beyond the Tempest

Nature yawns in restless sleep,
stirs Elmo's fire beneath the deep.
Storm, wind, angry sea,
Vulcan sparks catastrophe.
Hell is empty, all devils are here;
bold waves tremble, disaster draws near.
Paradise island above ocea'n lye,
earthquake provokes, tsunami samurai.

Obeisance to ancient world has stood,
from Solomon's temple to Noah's flood.
Innocent souls, with matter combine,
a faceless vision, the abyss of time.
For Ariel's sphere of illusion spins,
cyclonic mistral – demonic wind.
Sign of covenant, bow in the sky,
earthquake invokes, tsunami samurai.

Wild clouds carve in masquerading faces,
talismanic images etched, embraces
the realm of magic through the ages;
almighty God, wisdom of sages.
Kingdoms come, and kingdoms go,
even the bard and Prospero.
Spirited shadows fade and die,
earthquake evokes, tsunami samurai.

Back to reality, forward in time,
seismic activity, computer on line.
Explosive heat in ring of fire,
resonates through axis, daytime expires.
Genesis of warnings failed to contact,
genocide by nature, cold hard fact.
Nine zero magnitude by science decree,
earthquake provokes, another tsunami.

***Ron Nicola***

# Fighting Back
A 10 minute play for television

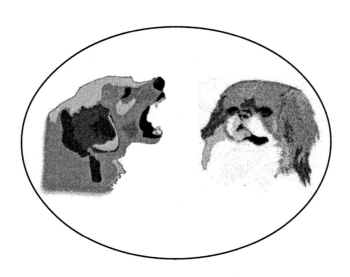

**Episode One**

**The Letter**

| | |
|---|---|
| GLENYS WALTON | Housewife |
| BERNARD WALTON | Retired Clerk |
| MAVIS | Check-out Girl |
| BEGGAR | |
| BUTCH | Beggar's Mongrel Dog |
| CHI-CHI | Waltons' Pekinese Dog |
| MRS. THOMPKINSON | Vicar's Wife |

**1. Int. supermarket day**

*Glenys and Bernard are shopping in the supermarket. Glenys is consulting her list. Bernard pushing trolley. He drops in the odd goodies unnoticed by Glenys. They hesitate at a stand.*

GLENYS Pass me a tin of salmon, Bernard.

*Bernard selects a tin*

GLENYS No, not the large one, the *little* one! We can pad it out with mayonnaise, she'll never know.

*Bernard sighs and puts it back. Glenys reaches for a large tin of baked beans.*

GLENYS That'll do nicely for the church raffle.

*They reach the check-out. Goods are rushed through. Glenys searches for her purse in large handbag. Bernard starts to pack.*

CHECKOUT GIRL That's £15.78 pence

GLENYS *(shocked)* Don't be so silly - I've next to nothing here!

CHECK-OUT GIRL *(crossly holding out receipt)* There's your till receipt to check.

GLENYS *(puts glasses on and studies list)* I've never picked up smoked oysters....Quails eggs? ...Give me that bag, Bernard. I'll show her!

*Bernard folds over top of one bag, looking shifty.*

BERNARD Er.. which one dear?

GLENYS *(comprehension dawning)* BERNARD! PAY!

*Impatient queue behind Glenys crane forward and snigger.*

BERNARD *(reaches for his wallet - mumbling)* Just a few little extras, dear.

GLENYS *(angrily pushes trolley at him)* That's the last time I get you to help me.

*They make for the exit.*


**2. Int. foyer, day**

*A woman with a collecting tin steps in front of them and holds tin up to Glenys*

COLLECTING LADY Anything for the Cats' Protection?

GLENYS *(shoves tin to one side)* The little blighters will need protecting if I catch them in my garden again!


**3. Ext. car-park day**

*They approach a beggar sitting on a newspaper. He has a large mongrel dog beside him.*

BEGGAR *(holding out his hand)* Spare a bob, lady?

GLENYS *(outraged)* Certainly not. Get off your backside and get a job.

*She pushes the trolley past him and 'accidentally' tips his collecting tin over with her foot.*

GLENYS (*astonished*) Would you look at that Bernard! More than we get in a week! What cheek!

*The dog growls and on-lookers give sour looks and drop more money in the tin in sympathy for the beggar.*

## 4. Int. kitchen. day

*Glenys and Bernard are unpacking carrier bags onto kitchen table. Pekinese dog begs for food*

GLENYS (*banging goods down on table*) Stilton cheese! Stilton! And Bath Oliver biscuits? If Mrs Thompkinson sees these she'll think we've come into money, and she'll *always* be after us for church donations.

*Sound off - knocking on front door. Dog rushes out of the room, yapping.*

GLENYS See who that is Bernard, and if it's anyone collecting, tell them to bugger off and start a collection for us.

*Bernard exits kitchen and returns holding several letters. He shuffles the letters around and holds up one with a large blue cross on it, c.u. of letter. He puts it at the back of the pile and lays them on the table.*

GLENYS (*without looking up and still sorting the groceries*) Well, who was it?

BERNARD (*meekly*) It was only the postman, dear.

GLENYS (*scowling at an extra large packet of dog biscuits*) But why did he knock? Is he too high and mighty to push them through the letter-box? Ever since you told him you'd retired he gives me a 'poor you' look. He's probably checking to see if you are still with us! (*archly*) He's always fancied me! (*smirks to herself, and opens a cupboard door*)

*Bernard bends down to stroke dog, who's jumping up at the smell of the biscuits.*

BERNARD (*to the dog*) He's well known for his fancy women!

GLENYS (*rolling her eyes at a tin of asparagus*) What did you say Bernard?

BERNARD (*nervously*) He had a recorded delivery which I had to sign for, dear.

GLENYS (*sarcastically*) Perhaps we've won the lottery - open it. Here you are Chi-Chi. (*she opens the box of dog biscuits and gives the dog a large bone-shaped one*)

BERNARD (*sliding the letter out of sight*) It's nothing dear, I'll deal with it later

GLENYS (*closing the cupboard door*) Put the kettle on, I want to drown my sorrows. (*she sits in a chair at the table*)

*Bernard starts towards the kitchen sink, accidentally knocks letters to the floor. Dog picks up blue cross letter. c.u. of letter, takes it to Glenys. Bernard puts hand to forehead and waits. Glenys opens letter. c.u. of letter shows final demand for Bernard's golf annual fee of £275.00*

GLENYS (*jumps up and shouts*) BERNARD! (*dog yaps*)

BERNARD (*visibly distressed*) Yes dear?

GLENYS (*with hands over face, wails*) Two hundred and seventy five pounds! Oh! Bernard, *how* are we going to pay it?

BERNARD (*contritely*) I'll give it up, dear. (*he puts a comforting arm around her*) I don't think I'm much good at it anyway, my handicap's still 35! (*He takes a clean handkerchief from his trouser pocket and offers it*)

GLENYS (*takes the handkerchief and dabs her eyes*) And you're my handicap Bernard Walton! You can't give it up. What will Mrs. Thompkinson think?

## 5. Int. sitting-room, day.

*Glenys stands in the middle of the room with hat and coat on.*

GLENYS (*looking towards hall door*) You can come out now Bernard

*Bernard appears in doorway dressed as a tramp. Has false grey beard and moustache and dirty face. Dressed in old mac, and flat hat, with hair spiking out, and wearing wellies. Dog's long hair dirty, has collar and lead of string. Bernard stands for moment in doorway with lead in hand, dog hangs head.*

BERNARD Don't you think this is a bit extreme dear?

GLENYS (*tartly*) Well no-one will recognise you, that's for sure! We have to fight back. You saw how much that disgusting man made. (*She bends to pat dog and recoils at the smell.*) I'll drive you there and I'll walk past every few minutes and throw 50 pence in.

BERNARD (*perplexed*) But wouldn't that defeat the object dear?

GLENYS (*exasperated*) You silly man, of course not. It will draw attention to you and encourage others to be generous.

## 6. Ext. supermarket car-park

*Bernard and dog are seen approaching same site as beggar. Bernard turns to look pleadingly at Glenys sitting in parked car. She urges him on with impatient wave of hand. Bernard puts down collecting box and makes dog sit beside him.*

*c.u. of box printed on side: 'Down with the Government - Support starving O.A.P'S'*

BEGGAR (*from side of mouth, angrily*) Piss off. This is my pitch,

BERNARD Sorry, old chap. It's more than my life's worth.

*Bernard's dog yaps at beggar's dog, which moves closer to beggar. Glenys walking by, pointedly drops 50 pence in Bernard's box .*

GLENYS (*hissing with teeth clenched*) For goodness sake - look hungry! (*she moves on*)

*Mrs. Thompkinson comes out of supermarket. Glenys spots her and hurries to head her away from Bernard.*

GLENYS (*she almost shouts*) MRS. THOMPKINSON! What a pleasant surprise!

*Mrs. Thompkinson waves and turns to walk towards the beggar. Glenys catches up with her.*

MRS. THOMPKINSON Must give him something. He's come to expect it. The church must be seen to be magnanimous.(*she turns to Bernard*) Oh dear! Now there's two of them. I was afraid that would happen. Word gets around you know. They'll have to have 25 pee each.. (*she rummages in her bag.*)

GLENYS But collecting for the Old Folk - a very good cause, don't you think? I think a pound would be right.

*Glenys very obviously drops money into Bernard's box. Mrs Thompkinson changes her mind C.U. of her hand as she drops 20 pence in beggar's tin and £1 coin in Bernard's tin. Beggar glowers at Bernard. Glenys raises finger to her lips to stop Bernard saying anything. Bernard, bemused by Glenys's donation, doesn't notice the gesture.*

BERNARD Thanks, Mrs T.

*Mrs Thompkinson bends forward to look under Bernard's cap*

MRS. THOMPKINSON (*fearfully*) Do I know you?

*Glenys creates diversion by kicking beggar's tin, spilling his money*

BEGGAR (*rising*) You silly cow. I know you - you did that yesterday! See to her Butch! (*he digs his reclining dog with his foot*)

*Beggar's dog starts barking. Bernard's dog yaps and bites beggar's dog. Beggar, Glenys and Mrs Thompkinson all shout at each other. Crowd gathers. Bernard and his dog slink away.*

## 7. Int. sitting-room - day

*Glenys, Bernard and Mrs. Thompkinson seated at tea table, Glenys passes a plate of delicate crustless sandwiches to Mrs. Thompkinson.*

GLENYS Do have a *Canadian* salmon sandwich. So much more tasty than those coarse red Russian ones.

MRS. THOMPKINSON (*takes a sandwich and stuffs the whole thing in her mouth.*) Wasn't that just too dreadful yesterday? Those evil-looking men, and ruffian dogs. I'm sure the church doesn't want to get involved with such wickedness. (*she looks directly at Bernard and scoffs*) Ha, what a laugh, I thought that tramp looked a bit like you! Now what old man would stoop so low? (*rising from the table*) Thank you for the tea, Glenys. I'm glad that you two are comfortably off. So, (*laughs coquettishly*) you won't mind me asking for (*wheedling voice*) a leetle something towards the church raffle?

GLENYS It's our pleasure, Mrs. Thompkinson. Go and get something Bernard.

*Bernard and dog exit room. Mrs. Thompkinson puts on her coat. Bernard reappears. C.u. of the exotic groceries as he places them on the table. Mrs. Thompkinson picks up one to examine it. Glenys glares at Bernard.*

MRS. THOMPKINSON (*in surprised tones*) Oh! How very generous! Asparagus, quails eggs - how wonderful! I knew I could rely on you for support. We'll put your name at the top of the donors' list.

GLENYS(*simperingly*) Go and get her the *tinned ham* Bernard

*Bernard goes off to the kitchen. followed by dog. N.O. a scuffle and yapping is heard.*

BERNARD (*o.o.v. shouting*) Chi-Chi! Come back you little beggar! Come back!

*The dog rushes into the sitting room. C.u. of the false beard and cap in its mouth. Bernard appears in the doorway looking stressed. Mrs Thompkinson looks from dog to Bernard. Realisation dawns.*

MRS. THOMPKINSON (*drops tin she is holding and with hands to face, screams*) Oh! No!

GLENYS (*anguished*) OH! BERNARD!

*Scene ends with Glenys and Mrs. Thompkinson looking at each other, one in embarrassment, the other in shock. Bernard bends to grab beard and cap from dog. Dog thinks it's a game, c.u. of dog chest down, tail up, wagging furiously.*

**Jean Russell-Parnell**

# Legend Writing Award

We would like to thank last year's six prizewinners for kindly agreeing to the inclusion of their stories in this anthology

### *The results were as follows:*

1st Yvonne Jackson *Eating Shrivelled Fruit*
2nd Anne Youngson *Under the Brim*
3rd Christine Buckland *A May Wedding*

### *Runners up:*

John Barfield *Thirty Different Words for Sand*
Alexandra Fox *Dead Leaves*
Monica Watson-Peck *Where Ocean Meets Lagoon*

These stories were chosen from a total of 362 entries

# Eating Shrivelled Fruit

The bus was running late again. This time it was some tiny piece of engine that was refusing.

Luckily, we Africans are smart, and know that these small problems can occur, so we take the precaution of employing a mechanic to travel on each bus. This time it was Akim, and for that I was happy, because he was that very same one who fixed the bus last September, so I know he is a good mechanic.

I watched Akim. He had removed the carburettor, taken from it all the pieces, and had laid them out in a line on the dusty road. Then he glanced at the sun, fetched his prayer mat from the bus, and began his devotions.

We passengers waited patiently, sitting or standing at the roadside. Two joined him in his prayers. The young woman next to me rocked gently and sang to her suckling baby. The old man with the goat walked it along the dusty highway, so that it could nibble what dry grass it could find. I was glad that goat had been at the other end of the bus because it was a very smelly animal and had defecated twice since leaving Nairobi. I do not think they should allow goats to travel on buses these days. After all, we are a modern society now, with television, Coca-cola, and mechanics to fix our buses. Even, I have a friend in Malaba town who lives in a house with a flushing toilet. Mostly running water is not there, so she has sensibly dug a long drop in the garden like everybody else, but when the water is on it is most wondrous. No, goats should stay where they belong, in the villages, and should not be taken on long journeys.

In my village there are now many goats, and most of them belong to my family. Even, we also have cattle, and our house has a roof of tin sheets. I am thankful that God has allowed me to bring this wealth to our home, with my job in Nairobi. There is even enough money to allow me to return home to Uganda twice a year, to see my five children. I am proud that I can pay for them all to go to school. Now that my husband is dead, my sister keeps them, along with her eight, and I know they will do well there, but I like to see them.

Grandfather says it is a waste of money, to make all these journeys backwards and forwards, but he has always remained at home, and does not know what it is to travel to a strange place. He cannot understand how my stomach feels like a hollowed out gourd when I think of the village. It is not like the city. The city is full of serious, hurrying strangers who do not greet each other.

As well as the goat, the bus had a second unusual passenger. It was a mzungu, a white man, quite young. This surprised me because these people usually travel by Landrover, as they all have much money. If they do not own a vehicle, they hire a taxi or travel by train. The train to the border has first class carriages where rich people can waste their money on soft mattresses for sleep and cooked food when they wake. But here was a mzungu on the same bus as a smelly goat! Such people do not like to do this kind of thing.

As we waited, he sat apart. I did not know why this should be and it saddened me. It is not natural for a person to be alone when there is company to be had. So I approached and greeted him.

'Praise God.'

He did not reply, 'Amen', as is our custom, so I knew him for a visitor, not living in Africa. He also passed over the other greetings, failing to enquire how I was, and whether all was fine at home and in the village. Such rudeness can be excused in a mzungu, as it is well known that they lack interest in such weighty matters, being only concerned with rushing here and there, attending to the many maintenance requirements of their money and possessions.

'I wonder how long we'll be stuck here,' he said.

'Do you?' It had not occurred to me to wonder about such a thing. Here in Africa, delays are part of the pattern of our lives and must be lived, not endured. I tried to encourage him.

'Akim is a good mechanic.'

He made a sound like a pig rooting.

'Look at him! He isn't even working on the problem.'

'He is attending to his spiritual life.'

'I can see.'

Such rudeness was puzzling. It occurred to me to attend to my own spiritual life, and I took a moment to pray for this graceless mzungu. I also prayed for the soul of Akim, whose spiritual zeal was sadly misguided, being directed towards the wrong god. Surely, the world is full of unsaved people, and the diligent prayers of Christians are much needed!

I withdrew a bunch of ripes from my bag and offered them to the youth. He took one of the tiny, sweet bananas.

'Thanks.'

Rummaging in his own bag, he produced a bag of shrivelled black things and offered them to me. I did not wish to give offence by refusing food, but I did not know what they were. Their appearance was like roasted ants, but larger. Summoning my manners, I reached into the bag and took two or three.

'Thank you. This is food from your place?'

'They're raisins. Dried grapes.'

'Grapes?'

'Oh – a fruit. Dried.'

I marvelled at the ways of the white man.

'Fancy eating shrivelled fruits when there are fresh ones to be had!' I exclaimed, then realising such a comment was ill-mannered, I quickly put the dried grapes into my mouth, to show him I had accepted his gift. They were chewy, but sweet, a strange, foreign taste.

The midday heat was heavy on us, although we all sat in the shade of the bus. We were awaiting the rainy season, and the sun had burned the world to dusty brown. The Rift Valley dropped away before us, and to either side of us the Trans-African Highway stretched distantly, lost in the shimmer. Vehicles were few at this time of day.

My mzungu friend glanced at his wristwatch.

'We're going to be terribly late.'

'We will arrive when it is time.'

'But we'll be late.'

'Late? For what event?'

He sighed and looked at his wristwatch again. His eyes were only attracted to that object. The whole beauty of Africa was displaying itself for his attention just below us, but he did not glance at it. He did not use the delay to improve his spiritual life, as Akim and the two passengers did, or to nourish another, as the young mother and the old man did. Even, he failed allow his body to take the rest a body requires, but made it jiggle and fidget, his eyes always returning to his wristwatch. The possession of such an item appeared to destroy his calm. It ruled over him and he writhed under its dictatorship.

'Someone is meeting me.'

- 135 -

'At Malaba?'

'At the border, yes. We'll be several hours late. She might have gone home.'

'But surely this person will wait? It is known that buses sometimes run late. For certain she will stay until you arrive.'

'Do you think so?' It seemed as if my words soothed his agitation.

'Even, I have somebody waiting for me at Malaba. It is my auntie. And if the bus delays to come, she will wait.'

'She will?'

'Yes. And if we arrive after the border is closed for the night, then – '

'Closed!'

He jumped up uselessly, walking this way and that, consulting the wristwatch once again.

'That it closes at six o'clock.'

'Six! Oh no! But it's four already!'

I was sad to see that I had made his condition worse. Even, I was afraid that he would become ill. There was no peace in him.

'Look.' I pointed to Akim. 'Our mechanic is now working. God willing we shall reach in time.'

The border opened at 6am. A mzungu lady greeted my young man.

'Rodney! You're late!'

'It was an awful journey. The wretched bus broke down. And the tyres! As bald as soap. The heat was really terrible. And the dust! I thought I'd never get here.'

He talked in jerks, such was his distress. I shook my head in wonder. These people! The proper greetings were not even there. His attitude was as shrivelled as his dried fruit. Then I saw Auntie.

'Auntie! Praise God!'

'Amen! How are you, Grace?'

'Even, I am fine. And you?'

'As for me, I am also fine.'

'The children?'

'They are well. How was the journey, Grace? That you delayed to come!'

I laughed.

'The journey was good. The bus was refusing, but Akim succeeded to mend it. And, Auntie, because of this small delay God blessed me with a new friend, a mzungu. Even, my friend Agatha kept us both at her house.

We had good fellowship. And by the grace of God there was running water, enabling us to use the toilet that flushes.'

Auntie rejoiced with me at my good fortune.

'God has indeed blessed you,' she observed, 'that He should make the bus run late again! Come, we shall go home.'

*Yvonne Jackson*

# Under the Brim

I'm hiding. I'm sitting here, hiding, under my hat. I like my hat. It reminds me of hot chocolate, I haven't a clue why, but there it is. It's probably something to do with when I got it, or where I got it. I forget. There are so many things I forget; I have to concentrate just to remember the things that are important.

It's raining outside so I'm hiding inside a bus shelter. It's the best bus shelter in the world. The walls are made of bricks that form a pattern and there are wooden beams in-between the pieces of the pattern. Solid. Strong word, strong bus shelter. There's a poster on the wall telling me when the buses come, but I can't read it. It doesn't matter, though, because I don't want a bus to come. I'm hiding.

If it weren't for the rain I would be outside in the bushes. I would prefer to be outside, but I can't be doing with the wet. It would spoil my hat. It would get everywhere. Water does that, have you noticed? It starts off in one place and before you have time to think it's everywhere else.

The person I'm hiding from is Little Miss Bossy. I'm staying at her house but I had to run away because I couldn't cope. She always says that: 'Oh, I just can't cope!' She never runs away, though, so I think she is coping. She even copes with her husband, who has halitosis, which is a very tasty word but not a nice thing. Personally I have always looked after my teeth. I couldn't cope with the noise in her house; the noise and the things which were going on - or going off or going up or going down or going sideways.

I wish it would stop raining, the wetness upsets me. Wet and words bother me, but not much else. I'm not worried about global warming or GM foods or terrorism. I'm not interested in clocks anymore, or sell by dates, or the News. I stopped bothering about the News when my husband died. I can't remember when that was, but it was a long time ago, and after that I didn't have to bother with the News any more. All men have to bother with the News, or I presume they have to because they all do. Old Smelly Breath is just the same as my husband used to be.

'It's time for the News!'

'Oh no, I've missed the News. Remind me to catch it at 9 o'clock.'

Perhaps they feel they owe it to all the other men, who go out and find the News and make it into programmes, to watch what they've done. Perhaps they're worried that something will happen which everyone else will know about and they won't and they'll never be able to admit they don't know and they'll never be able to take part in a conversation which has anything to do with this event, ever again. It would be like missing the lesson where they taught you multiplication and never being able to find out how to do it.

Oh no, now the wet has come in here with me. I think I may have done a wee. It's all the rain, and thinking of something else. Yes, I have. I'd better mop the bench with my skirt so it doesn't run off into my wellies. It's a good skirt. It's dark blue and quite thick so it won't show a bit of pee. It used to have elastic round the waist but that seems to have given out so I hold it up with a belt. I've a feeling someone made me the skirt, but I have no idea where the belt came from. Perhaps the lady next door gave it to me. I'll never know now because she's moved away. I don't know where and I don't know why. I've never understood why people move; I like my house, I belong there. I don't worry about anything when I'm at home.

Now my face is wet. Where did that come from? It could be the rain or having a wee or the pipes might be leaking. There's just too much of it about. It just keeps coming from somewhere and going everywhere else.

Here are some of the other things I have stopped worrying about: What People Think, Underwear, Locks.

I'm rather pleased my neighbour moved because I have a new one now and she is nice. She is called Amy which sounds like a sigh. I could go to sleep in her hair. She will go to the shop for me to buy food. I can't go any more because the lady in there won't let me. She's a hard one, not like Amy. I think her boobs are made of concrete because they never move whatever she does and she creases all her features up when she looks at me then smoothes them out again. She looks like a balloon with the air going in and out. She calls my wellies gumboots. They may be the problem, I don't know. Perhaps if I bought a nice pair of brown lace-ups she would let me in. I don't want to go in, though, because I have this problem with my eyes where I can't see things very clearly and it is very confusing in there. Amy will go for me, I'm sure she will. She has such a nice name and hair like a duvet.

It's annoying about my eyes. Most of me works really well. My legs work and my knees work and I've got both my tits and all my insides. Little Miss

Thing made me go to Day Centre once - well four times actually. Why is it called a Day Centre? If I wanted a Centre to my Day it would be my house, not a horrid hall which wasn't even as nice as this bus shelter. The people who had this hall at the centre of their day could none of them stand up or sit down or walk as well as I can.

I have no problem with my hearing, either, but that's a secret. I have to pretend I can't hear or the talking would drive me mad. The eyes are a secret too. I don't want anyone to know I can't see because I know what they'd think. And I can look after myself, it's only that my eyes don't always recognise what they're looking at, and my bladder forgets to tell me when it's full.

I feel safe in here, in this bus shelter. I like the way the bricks are all sitting neatly next to each other.

The talk bothers me. They use words like 'awful' and 'careful' and 'money' and 'expected' and 'worry'. Money is another thing I don't worry about. Sometimes they ask questions. That's the worst. 'Do you, won't you, can't you, why don't you, why can't you - ?' I never listen to the end so I don't know what to answer.

Hang on, is that a bus? It sounds like . . . No, it's only a big van. I didn't want it to be a bus. The driver would have looked at me and spoken to me. I would have had to say I don't want to catch a bus and he would probably have said, 'What are you doing sitting at a bus stop, then?' as if everything had to fit into a pattern. And I wouldn't know what to say in return, because I wouldn't want to explain, so I would most likely say something like 'Hiding' and he would reply, 'Not a good place for that!' as if he was the world's expert on hiding and knew all the five-star places.

Still, it wasn't a bus and I didn't have to talk to anyone. I can't keep up with all the talking. I don't want to keep up. I used to listen, in the old days when my husband was alive and my children were at home. I think it was my job to listen. They all wanted something and I had to listen to find out what it was they wanted so I could give it to them. I always understood what they wanted then but now I don't understand what they want and whatever it is I never seem to get it right. And Little Miss B says, 'Oh, Mum, why don't you ever listen?' I don't want to listen any more. I want silence. I want words only to be in my head or on a piece of paper. I like them then. I like words. I particularly like words with lots of syllables and odd consonants where you don't expect them. Hebdomadal, for instance. That's a chunky word. Fishbone. That's OK. Cataclysm. That's one of my favourites. I use these words sometimes when I haven't understood what they've said but they want me to say something back.

Too many words and too much water. I used to be wet all the time, when it was my job to look after everyone. Everything had to be washed: clothes, dishes, floors, children, hands, hair, paintwork, car, ornaments, baths, basins, worktops. I bobbed along all right at the time; I don't remember whether I was happy but I was afloat. Now I think I'm drowning, the words are weighting me down and the water is carrying me away.

They want to put me in a Nursing Home. That's the truth, that's what I'm hiding from. They think that because I don't care about all the important things like the News and money and dust and I can't be bothered with listening to their words, I must be incapable of boiling my own kettle and making my own cup of tea in my own house. I hear them talking about it because they think I'm deaf and I'm not. They keep using the word Home. Such a nice word. H and M are two of my favourite letters. My home is where I'm happy.

I should be worried about what to do next, but if I concentrate maybe this moment in the bus shelter will go on for ever. Some moments do. I have some moments in my memory which I can feel still going on when I think about them. Only I can't think of any just now.

I particularly like this bus shelter. And I like the way the brim of my hat makes a shape round the doorway.

Actually, I decided to run away because of the water. I forgot to wake up when I needed a wee in the night and I thought if they knew it would start them talking again, so I put the sheets in the bath and then I forgot what I was doing and started wondering how to spell 'miscellany' and I only noticed that the bath was running over when my slippers were wet. So I put on my hat and my wellies and my big blue skirt and I ran away to this bus shelter.

I think I'm in a bit of a mess. I think I am a mess, actually. 'What a mess!' they'll say when they find me.

I'd go home if I could, but I don't know how to find home from here.

*Anne Youngson*

# A May Wedding

Lottie was ten when Miriam, her elder sister, married Saul, her childhood sweetheart. At the engagement party she was told by a well-meaning relative that she would soon be calling him 'brother-in-law'. She was shocked. He was nothing like Benjie or Aaron, her brothers. Saul was so old, so serious and dressed like Father. He never told jokes or played games like Benjie did. He always had money jangling in his pockets and smelled of cigarettes and cigars. Intrigued, as well as horrified, Lottie took to observing Saul with an immense, detached, curiosity from then on. She noticed what he wore, what he talked about and how important he seemed.

Everyone listened when Saul spoke, even Father, who usually did most of the talking in their house. Mother was mesmerised by Saul and hovered around the Sabbath table offering him the choicest morsels and the largest portions of pudding. Lottie stared at him through the candlesticks and wondered what had transformed the rather dull boyfriend into a demi-god. She found herself pondering on so many things, as if she had found the last piece of the jigsaw but then realised it wouldn't fit. How could Miriam bear to give up the cosy world of their family for a new life with Saul in a strange home? It just did not make sense. On Saturday evenings, when he left their house, he usually pressed a few pfennigs rather awkwardly into her hand and although that pleased her, just a tiny bit, she had to put up with her hair being ruffled by him and she didn't like that at all.

Saul was a businessman, something connected with Father's factory so they did not see much of him, or Father, during the week. At weekends he came with gifts for them all and a wallet full of notes. Benjie and Aaron buzzed around him, fascinated, secretly spiriting away half-smoked cigars which they inhaled until they vomited, whilst Miriam metamorphosed into a vague, gauzy creature who wafted dreamily in and out of the morning room in a cloud of exotic and sometimes overpowering perfume.

Lottie hated the way things changed when Saul came in through the door. She hated the formality of her parents, their lack of spontaneity; the unknown plot and script that everyone else seemed to keep to, whilst she felt increasingly lost somewhere on the margins of their grown up world.

Things could only get worse and they did. Whilst Saul became more and more important in the Beckermann household, Lottie felt herself growing smaller and smaller. She began to test her theory out and took to missing meals at the weekends just to see if anyone noticed. Sometimes her Mother would come looking for her but the nearer it got to the May wedding no one remembered her and she would, eventually, creep down to the kitchen and ask cook for left-overs or else make do with milk and biscuits.

When Saul was absent she would scamper through the house, running into her sister's room, snuggling into her empty bed and playing with Miriam's old dolls, the precious ones which had not been handed down to her. She would write notes, secret messages for her sister and hide them in the pockets of her work suits and imagine Miriam's expression when she read them in the office. She would cut pictures out of her sister's Brides' magazines imagining that Miriam would never be able to order a gown if she couldn't find a picture of one she liked, and then being dismayed, one Sunday evening, when Mrs Goldblum arrived to take Miriam's measurements and to discuss fabrics.

'Lottie, Lottie dear, we want you in Miriam's room right now!' her Mother called in a prickly, strained voice. She thought of going out for a ride on her bicycle but her Father passed her in the hallway just at the moment her Mother called down again and she had no choice but to clump, clump, and clump up the stairs, her head hanging down and her ribbon straggling, half undone.

Much later she remembered how Miriam's room had seemed all lit up; the electric light reflecting off the bales of white fabric and trimmings. It had surprised her. For a moment Lottie stood in the doorway, shyly and gawkily observing the women earnestly disputing the merits of organza, crêpe de chine, moiré satin and silk damask. They were speaking a rare, foreign language which she could not comprehend. The words seemed to separate her even further from them, as if she was observing it all from beyond, outside their frame of belonging.

They began to remove Lottie's clothing and she struggled when her hair ribbon caught in the zip of her grey school tunic and tugged her scalp so painfully she cried out. They prodded her and measured her and talked over the top of her head. There were no pfennigs, either, so it was much worse than having to put up with Saul. They decided on mauve for her and

- 143 -

beamed at her expectantly but she made no response because she had never heard the word before and did not know it meant dark lilac, which was a colour she loved. She dressed sullenly; her mouth was disagreeable, her cheeks hot. Her Mother sighed heavily when she left the room and Miriam raised her eyes to the ceiling, tut-tutting dramatically at her little sister's peevishness.

The day of the wedding arrived too soon. They all had to fast from first light. That wasn't a problem for Miriam, who had been dieting since the day of Mrs Goldblum's visit when her measurements were made public by her Mother at the dinner table. She was now svelte and slender in a way Lottie felt was unfamiliar and unlovely. Her cheekbones were too prominent and her breastbone and shoulders appeared angular and harsh under the softness of her oyster wedding gown. Lottie noticed the rustle and swish of her own dress but thought little more of it for her stomach rumbled throughout the ceremony and she was mortified by embarrassment.

They were outside in the garden underneath the apple blossom. Teams of men had been working for weeks to coax the garden into something even greater than its usual May glory of camellias, magnolias, and apple blossom. Lottie remembered for years afterwards the pink flowers that had fallen onto Miriam's train and settled on the Chuppah, the velvet embroidered canopy, under which the young couple stood together to be married.

She understood little of the ceremony after the first words: *He who is mighty, blessed and great above all beings, may He bless the bridegroom and the bride'* for, at that time, she did not understand Hebrew. She was startled back to life when Saul crushed the glass under his heel and she whispered to her Aunt Esther, 'Why has he done that? Is he angry?'

'No child,' her aunt replied, her voice soothing, gentle and kindly: the kindest voice she had heard since Miriam announced to their world that she was marrying Saul. 'It is a symbolic act, which means it shows that when Saul crushes the glass he expects there will be times of sorrow as well as joy in his marriage to your sister.' Aunt Esther bent down and smiled at her as she carefully removed the pink apple blossom petals which had stuck to her hair.

The last time she had seen Miriam she had been wearing her work-camp clothes. They hung round her thin frame, her shoulder blades poking cruelly through the rough fabric. She had been reaching out to the apple blossom tree beyond the perimeter fence when the guards had knocked her over.

There were no more May weddings for the Beckermann family. She found the single, once-pink petal caught in the skirts of her mauve best dress. The petal was brown now and quite crispy and fragile, like the dress. She brought the fabric up to her face and breathed in the smell, hoping to capture the familiar scent of home, of family. It smelled of ashes. There was little else worth retrieving from the debris that had been their family's home. She did not stay long.

*Christine Buckland*

# Thirty Different Words for Sand

It was seven days since Khorosh, last of the wizards, had killed his lover. From the balcony of his red marble fortress he stared at the ruins of Hassim's tower, where the desert turned to glass. The morning light glistened off it like fiery dew, so bright it hurt the eyes, but he did not look away. He sat on the only chair, drank mint tea from the only cup and was content.

A sudden breeze blew the thin layer of sand on the balcony floor into a dust-devil. He shielded his eyes and when the wind had passed he saw a woman leaning back against the railings. Her skin, her silken clothes, the jewellery she wore, all were the colour of sand. He didn't have to look at her face to know that it was Alia.

'Why did you kill me?'

He sipped his mint tea, realised it was cold and called for his servant.

'Why, Khorosh? I know you loved me.'

Fire flashed from his fingertips and the sand forming the apparition was instantly fused into a thin shell of glass. It toppled over, shattering into a million pieces on the marble floor.

A servant appeared in the doorway, bowed low.

'Mahmoud, more tea. And clear up this mess. I will be in the garden.'

The courtyard garden had been one of Alia's projects. Pots of earth were arrayed around the walls and climbing roses embraced trellises, bringing colour and life to the castle. Already the roses had begun to die, unwatered and uncared for. But it was not the roses he had come to see.

In the middle of the bare sand floor was a single white stone. It bore her name, the date of her death, and symbols he had inscribed to ensure she remained dead. For when dealing with a witch, especially one he had trained himself and who had come to rival him in power, these things should never be left to chance.

When he arrived, she was already there. 'All this to stop me rising *up* out of my grave. But I knew the thirty different words for sand so I just went *sideways,* my spirit dispersing through the desert.' She lifted a drooping rose, tried to tuck it back into the trellis, then gave up with a sigh. 'I'm not a vengeful person,' she said, 'but you had me killed, Khorosh. Doesn't that demand revenge?'

As Alia spoke, Mahmoud entered the garden from the door behind her and at the wizard's slightest nod drew a knife from his sleeve. At the last moment, she must have heard him. She span around but was too late to dodge the blow. The blade pierced her stomach, Mahmoud's whole forearm disappearing after it into the sand. With a look of horror on his face, he snatched it hurriedly back.

Like a footprint filled in by the desert wind, the hole slowly closed. Within a few seconds all that remained was a tiny slit, sand trickling to the floor. Then even that stopped and Alia looked up at Mahmoud, her flat sand eyes revealing nothing, her voice even less. 'You've done that once before. Don't imagine I've forgotten.'

She turned back to the wizard. 'I know you loved me. You told me that magic can't change time, but if you had it over, could you kill me again?'

He raised his hand, hesitated a second. 'You stole something from me,' he told her. 'You had to die.' Then he scourged her once more with flame, the sound of breaking glass echoing through the sterile marble halls.

She didn't visit him for a week. Then one day, the shutters blew open, sand blew in and there she was, perched on the edge of his desk, holding one of his quills.

'Good morning, my lover.'

'Mahmoud,' he yelled, 'more tea!'

'You can't pretend I'm not here. Oh, and you'll have to make your own tea from now on. Mahmoud had an accident. He stepped in some quicksand in the garden.'

Khorosh's mask dropped, just for a second, and fire fused Alia in place. The glass figure toppled backwards, out of sight, but the sound of its shattering told him all he needed to know.

Almost at once, the dust-devil arose again and she was back, leaning against the wall, toying with the ornate hourglass and ignoring the interruption. 'The same thing happened to the camels bringing your food and water a couple of days ago. The Bedouin were able to flee but the supplies were lost. When I said I'd take my revenge, I didn't say I'd fight you directly, even in death I'm not that stupid. And it should be obvious by now, even to one as stubborn as you, that you cannot destroy me either. Not even Hassim the great could destroy me. I'm in every grain of sand in this desert.'

He sat back, and glared at her, his fingers constantly stretching out and pulling back into a fist.

'I know why you killed me, Khorosh.'

He frowned, his thoughts suddenly in very unwizardly disarray. *How can she know why I killed her, when I am not even sure myself?*

'But just say you loved me, say you would take it back if you could and maybe, just maybe, I could rest.'

He didn't answer, just frowned. *What was it she said? Not even Hassim the Great could destroy me, I'm in every grain of sand in this desert?* And suddenly he had an idea. He rose from his chair, strode to a table and frantically began to pick up and discard scroll after scroll. Their ancient parchment was discoloured yet they smelled not of mould, but of power, heady as a draught of the finest wine.

'What are you looking for Khorosh?' She sounded nervous. 'You don't have any spells that could harm me; no spells that could affect an entire desert.'

But Khorosh had found the scroll he was looking for. He placed it on his desk and carefully unrolled it. Alia approached, turned her head to one side to read it and recoiled. 'Hassim's invocation!' She glanced out the window to where the desert turned to glass around the ruins of Hassim's tower. 'Either you're bluffing or you're mad!'

Khorosh stared at her impassively.

'Even the greatest sorcerer couldn't control that spell. It consumed him. Maybe you were a powerful wizard once, but even in your prime you were no Hassim.'

'We shall see.' His fire lashed out again, fused and shattered her image. Sand blasted in from the desert, blinding him, but his flames fought it back, until the air cleared and he could close the shutters, throw the bolts and be alone at last.

And so Khorosh, last of the wizards, settled down in his high-backed chair to begin the reading of Hassim's invocation. It was a simple spell; thirty words in all. Those not steeped in the dark arts would have struggled over them, not knowing why they stuttered, not knowing why they could not pronounce the simple words. Such problems did not trouble Khorosh.

But casting the spell once was not the challenge. It must be repeated and repeated again, its power building with every recitation. And to do what he planned would take a whole hour. The tiniest slip, the smallest mispronunciation and the energies would rebound on him. Khorosh's red marble fortress would be just another shattered ruin like Hassim's, nothing more than a waypoint for the desert caravans, its lone occupant completely devoured by his own magics.

Turning over the hourglass, he began to read. It was easier than he'd thought. A relief, but as the hour wore on, he knew it would get harder, much harder.

He crossed to the eastern window, peered between the shutter's slats to see the sun had just crested the dunes. *'I remember when this was all sand,'* the nomads would tell their children. That was if any survived the impending conflagration, fleeing the desert to the barren, rocky ground beyond. *They'll probably invent thirty different words for glass.* And with that thought, he locked down the shutters all around the room.

She thought he wasn't the equal of Hassim? He would show her what true power was, and in so doing, he would destroy her. Then an, odd thing happened. For a fleeting moment, the prospect of Alia's destruction didn't seem an entirely a good thing. He remembered the good times he had spent with her, teaching her magic. And he remembered the first time they had made love . . . and the last time.

*What am I thinking?*

He had a spell to cast. A wonder that he hadn't skipped a syllable, flattened a vowel or stuttered on a tricky consonant. Was this what had happened to Hassim, distracted one second and gone the next? A chill went through him and he concentrated on the words to the exclusion of all else.

He glanced at the hourglass. Little time had passed and he began to pace around the room as he recited the spell, willing the hour to pass him by. Each time his orbit took him past the desk he glanced at the hourglass again but each time the top portion was depressingly full and he set it from his mind, watching instead the fiery flashes slipping through the joints of the shutters.

The same words he had repeated so easily at the beginning of the hour were becoming so hard to remember, so hard to pronounce. He stood breathlessly chanting in the centre of the room, drained by the relentless and growing pressure.

*Still half full!*

The remaining time passed in pain and delirium. He concentrated on keeping up the chant, keeping the spell going, but now there were flashes of fire in his mind to rival those in the sky outside. It seemed to last forever, but at last he turned to find the hourglass empty.

With a scream of pain, he fell to the floor, managed to crawl to the balcony door and pull it open. The scene outside was far worse than he had intended. Where before there had been dunes, now a flat cauldron of bubbling, multi-coloured glass stretched from horizon to horizon. The noon desert sun reflected off its surface, setting barbs in his eyes, and he looked away in agony.

Only now, when all the sand was gone, and Alia gone along with it, did he finally realise why it was she had to die. 'I am Khorosh, last of the wizards,' he croaked and for the first time in a long while, it was unreservedly true. '*You stole something from me. You had to die,*' he had told her, not realising how literally he had spoken. She had stolen his uniqueness.

'Khorosh, last of the wizards,' he repeated more slowly, savouring each syllable; but when he reached inside, to that place from which he had always drawn his magic, his triumph turned to ashes. Alia had not been far wrong when she said the spell would consume him. All that remained inside was a burned and cauterised stub. His uniqueness was gone again; spent in one vain act and with a sick feeling he realised that had been her plan all along.

He had thought just an hour had passed but the sun was straight overhead, so it must be nearer three! No wonder the spell had cost him so dearly. How could he have made such a basic error? He had watched the hourglass almost constantly.

And then it hit him. *Magic cannot alter time* he had told Alia, but she had proved him wrong. Under her sorcery, the sand in the hourglass had fallen slowly, tricking him into over-reaching himself, burning himself out. And from that sand, Alia's face regarded him with pity. Then it was gone forever, leaving his impotent cries to echo around the lonely marble halls.

*John Barfield*

# Dead Leaves

There are wires wrapped around the post, their ends twisted tight by bleeding fingers. There's string fast-knotted, and green garden twine. Nails have been banged in, half-buried, and where they've rusted in the rain brown streaks trickle down the cracked concrete. It's all hung with the flapping bunting of dead leaves, and the same wind that lifts them stirs the branches of the great copper beech tree. Handfuls of drying leaves move across the light, illuminating a circle in jaundice yellow, then flashing dark-red-dark again.

I came here first at daffodil time, tucked a yellow trumpet of hope into the ring, found it dashed on the floor next morning. Roses, irises, dahlias, I worked my way through the year, each bloom a hand of friendship tentatively outstretched. Now I bring a chrysanthemum, its furled petals heavy with sour death-scent. I snipped it from its plant earlier this evening, cut it from the succour of its root. I tuck it gently into the coil of wire around the post, and its head droops.

I should have brought a mat or an extra coat to sit on. My skirt will wick the dampness from the ground. It doesn't matter. I sit on the grass, just beyond the wash of the streetlight. The children are asleep in bed. This time, at last, I'm going to wait. This has gone on long enough; it's time for an accounting.

What time of night is it when you throw away my gesture, Janice, pull away your hand as you see the very thought of mine approaching, pull the petalled head from its stem and drop it on the ground? Is it now, when you know Sammy's safe in bed, when you've poured yourself a drink and sat down, and there's nothing but that great grey box in the corner to whisper vapidities at you? Is that when you feel the house crackle around you in wrapping-paper emptiness, uselessness, and you have to walk, to *do something*, go somewhere, take one step back towards her, to take my hand, my wave, nod, kiss of friendship, flower, and tread it into the mud. I know. I understand so very well.

I've worn a path, Janice, walking down the verge towards this spot. Is there a matched set of footprints stretching in the other direction?

Maybe it's in the small hours that you come, in the cool tomb of the night, three o'clock, when the village falls under a Midwich spell and nothing moves. Is that when you open your front door, and step alone into the darkness, just alive against the black-and-white backdrop of a silent movie, walking through her vacuum?

Janice, I haven't forgiven him. I never will, can.

I won't have him back when they let him out.

It was the excuses that finished it for me, his 'I was only just over the limit, just an extra glass or two,' his 'why can't the police leave me alone and concentrate on real criminals? There's nothing wrong with having a drink.' It was his feet slipping on the brake, the sun being in his eyes, the thirty-mile-an-hour limit at the bottom of the hill just to catch law-abiding drivers and make money out of them. He saw it as some sort of class war, police against *his* type, that there should be different laws for the Oxbridge men, those who could "carry their drink".

If he had said just once that he couldn't close his eyes any more, that his eyelids were imprinted with your Sarah's body smashed open on the road, her legs twisted, brain spilling from the shell of her skull. He never admitted that he could hear her voice in his own daughter's loneliness, that his wheels had carved a gouge through his family, friends, everybody he ran into.

Janice, you've no idea what life with him was like. You saw the public Mark, the cheerful chappie, the good egg. You might've seen a flash sometimes at parties, as his eyes narrowed, changed their focus and I took him home. My God, you've no idea.

I was packing his stuff away today, into boxes. His CDs are all in broken cases, crushed beneath his drunken stumbling, books are torn where he threw them by their covers. His wardrobe sighs a whisky breath; I found vomit-splashed shoes on the floor at the back.

He wrecked me, Janice. For twenty years I've had the bait and switch, the Jekyll in the morning, oh-so-sorry for everything, forgive me, don't leave me, it'll never happen again . . . and the Hyde at night.

It wasn't the physical stuff that hurt, the deep pinches that showed how foul my fat was, the whacks around the head that bruised beneath the hair, the pushes into doorways, crabwalking me into the walls, forcing himself into my dry unwantingness with a pounding, drunken pounding and thrusting and everlasting tearing because he was too drunk to perform but he was going to get himself off if it killed him and I was there to be pounded at, an empty, useful, unattractive *hole.*

It was what he said, and what he honestly meant that hurt me, that he only stayed with me because I was *useful,* that nobody else would ever want me, that he was doing me a favour keeping me, that I was stupid, ugly, without talent or potential. Oh God . . . I hated him. As it got closer to his coming home each evening my stomach would squeeze, twist in on itself, bleed acid upward into my mouth; I'd clench, waiting, wondering what would step out of that car, what it would say, do. I'd hide the children. Didn't you ever wonder why Becky came over to play with Sarah so often?

He hasn't touched me with affection for fifteen years.

I'm sorry, Janice. I'm so sorry for your loss, your grief, your emptiness. What can I say?

Did you know your Sammy's being cruel? Did you know Becky's got no friends now, and the notes I take out of her pockets when I wash her school trousers make me gag and cry? Did you know that Joe's drinking? On his own, cider, beer, at fifteen. He thought he loved your Sarah. First love hurts, doesn't it?

Janice, what can I do? I've written to you. You used to slam the phone down if you heard my voice. Now you've changed your number.

I miss you.

You were my only real friend, the only one I talked to. We were in antenatal classes together, for Christ's sake. With Sarah and Becky, yes, I know. I've betrayed you, not telling you the truth, letting you think my life was good ... perhaps I was ashamed, boasting, trying to make you think my husband, my children, were better than yours. If you only knew how much I envied you, deep down.

Is everybody's life like this? If you peel back the covers, is the sheet stained underneath, crusted, coiled with wiry hairs, springs poking through ready to bruise, to catch, to rip?

Oh, Janice. Meet me this one time. Leave just one of my flowers in the twisted crown of thorns. Let me give Sarah just one small memorial, in memory of her giggle, her fake American accent when she played with Barbies, her lumbering on the dance-mat. She was in our bathroom when she started her first period. She came to me and asked me what to do. Yes. She trusted me.

And I knew, I knew. I should've taken away his keys, informed on him, told the police that my drunk husband was as lethal as a loaded gun in the hands of a vindictive child. But I didn't.

Janice. I'm going to sit here all night, and wait for your coming.

Please meet me, see me, talk - just a few words to release us both from this extra weight, this pain. We're moving away from here next week, going up north where we can afford to live. I won't be around any more like an irritating splinter stuck under your fingernail.

I hope you find peace. I'm sorry.

*Alexandra Fox*

# Where Ocean Meets Lagoon

I see him every morning when I walk the beach. Up where the milk wood and scrub fray into the sand he crouches amongst the dark tangle of branches, a face as withered and black as the dried-up acacia pods above his head. He just sits there staring at some distant point, the horizon perhaps.

'Morning,' I call out, but the crash of the ocean drowns out my voice. Sometimes I wave as I pass along the water's edge, but the light is so bright he doesn't see me, doesn't even turn his gaze.

One morning I leave the shoreline and struggle up to where he sits. 'A lovely day,' I say, wishing at once that I hadn't. Such a British state of mind; such a worthless comment in a country like this. Maybe he won't answer, maybe he only speaks Afrikaans, you can never tell.

His black face scrunches into a wide gummy smile, eyes. like mine, hidden in the dark of glasses. I don't need to see them to tell he is old, older even than me.

'All days are lovely here, my friend.' And he stares past my shoulder at the tide coming in hard and fast.

'I see you here every morning,' I say, keen to keep the words flowing. Since arriving here I've had little chance to talk, had even begun regretting I'd come, that I'd listened to friends back home with all their words of advice. 'Three years is too long, Samuel, you have to try and get over the shock. Maybe move away, or at least take a holiday.'

Such throwaway lines; so little to do with truth.

'And you too, my friend, have been here most mornings,' the old man says, still looking out at the horizon as if searching for something, a fishing boat perhaps.

'Yes. Best time of day before the suns too high. My wife and I used to travel a lot but never to hot countries like this ...' The words shrivel in my mouth. How long has it been since I have spoken of Freya? I'm surprised at how easily her name has slipped into our conversation.

Laughter ripples down the far end of beach; a huddle of canvas chairs are draped in tanned bodies, children jump the waves.

'How normal life can be for some,' the old man murmurs, and I wonder if he sees how long I've been away from normal.

'You're watching something out there with great interest, do you mind me asking what it is?'

His acacia-pod face smiles. 'I am listening to the melody of ocean, to the song of the air.'

I swallow and shift uneasily at his words, not what I had been expecting. A vague memory unravels. A young man in white toga talking to Freya at Paris airport, and me at the other end of the arrival hall changing pounds into francs, wondering what he was up to, begging for money no doubt.

'Was that fellow annoying you?' I asked on my return.

She laughed. 'He wanted to show me how to find the song in my heart.'

'A crazy man in a bed sheet!'

'A little eccentric maybe,' she replied, ignorant of how crazy eccentric could sometimes be.

And now this ancient hippy, who I've never met before, trying to tell me about songs in the air.

'Must be getting back for breakfast,' I say, feeling the familiar pain in my head take hold. And I walk back across the sand as briskly as my old legs allow.

The main street of town hunkers between the beach and my rented room. Not yet eight and already old rusted vans are pulling up, men unloading boxes of guava and mango; loud talk in a guttural language that spits out an English word now and then, surprising me when I understand snippets of conversation. A few locals stand in a huddle on the corner. Under a broad jacaranda a woman sits amongst a purple haze where the tree has dropped its blossom; so still and silent, like she's been there forever.

Breakfast always at the same café, beneath a flowering gum, talking to no one. The bustle of customers keeps my mind occupied; the waiter lets me stay on, sipping mugs of tea, sweet and hot as if drenched in sun and honey.

Sometimes I listen in on other tourists' conversations, the flicker of memory rekindled in a sulphurous glow. Like a snapshot I'll suddenly see a lake or field with Freya beside me, the sway of her dress caught by the wind and camera. Then the image blurs, thoughts tangle in a confused mess. Now the only memory I can be certain of is that we never saw Paris together, never got beyond that airport.

'Severe shock. It can play such strange games,' my doctor keeps saying. 'Give it time - it'll all come back to you when it's ready.'

Over three years. How long does a memory need to come home?

The local museum is around the corner, my daily refuge from the heat, a way to spend some hours before my afternoon nap. Its warren of shuttered rooms now so familiar, the overhead fans brumming noisily as I step inside.

Carved wooden boxes, bead necklaces and books, yellowed and faded behind dusty panes of glass; a small cabinet in the corner I've not noticed before with an open album of old photos, men holding guns, one with his foot and rifle butt resting on a dead tiger as if it's already a rug by his fireplace back in England. Then another photo, so different from the rest, of a couple standing on a verandah, the young man's arm wrapped tightly around the woman, something in her face so unsettling, a dimpled cheek, blue eyes peeking from beneath an old-fashioned straw hat. As I lean forward to take a closer look the walls seem to sway. I have to hold onto the cabinet to keep from falling.

Must be the heat, or the smell, so heady and stale. Like old paper and dead flowers; the scent of unstoppered memories.

I tell myself I just need to go back and rest; get away from this day that's too hot for its own good.

I am trying to flag down a taxi outside the airport. Freya stands somewhere behind me although I can't be sure until I hear the groan. Sometimes in these harrowing dreams the sound is so loud I wake with a churning stomach, fear punching the breath from my lungs. Other times her groan is barely audible, my eyes don't even flicker behind sleeping lids.

The dream is always the same after that. Freya sprawled on the ground, hands clutched to her chest, face so contorted. And in the distance, that flash of white toga. No shouts, no cries, just me standing helplessly as I watch her life drain away; rivulets of blood seeping into concrete pavement.

Outside, a car horn blasts in the street. My eyes open to the bronze patina of late afternoon, wet with sweat, the cotton bed sheet twisted around me in a tight cocoon. I stare at the ceiling fan, my heart still thudding from the dream. She hasn't been in my sleep for so long I have to squeeze my eyes shut to stop the tears.

My memory is dead; even her features are blurred in my mind, the detail of our years together, gone. And yet in my dreams I relive that day over and over, see the newspaper headlines so clearly: *English Housewife Stabbed by Religious Fanatic.*

A man in white toga who said he'd find the song in her heart. Stabbed her instead. And barely a mention of me in all those papers, the husband who failed to save her, the man who wished he'd been the victim instead. Left with nothing but loneliness and a lost memory. What's the point of finding it anyway?

Ochre light fills the air, twilight hovering, not yet convinced of nightfall. The sand is hard and rippled where the tide has slipped away, the walk to the river mouth quicker than usual.

'Again you are here. Come up my friend and join me.'

I'm surprised to see him still sitting there, hadn't noticed anyone in the muted light. I stop by the tide line, wondering what to do. Can't just vanish into the ocean before his very eyes, yet I'm in no mind for his unsettling talk. I sigh, realise I have no choice and slowly make my way up to where the wild camphor brushes against the dunes.

'Here, sit down, keep me company.' And he pats the mat of undergrowth beside him. 'You look tired.'

Tired of life, I think, leaning against the trunk of an acacia, lowering myself slowly to the ground.

'Listen with me,' he whispers. 'Listen to the sweet notes in the air.'

And I groan and think, not again for God's sake, suddenly wondering if this was how Freya felt that day; wishing she could tell the white toga to get lost, to leave her in peace. Was she unnerved by his talk, the way I now feel?

"For it helps when the sadness of years comes upon me,' he goes on, ignoring my groan. 'Or when I need the sight my eyes have lost.'

I shoot a sideways glance. see he's still wearing sunglasses and a rush of guilt sweeps over me for thinking so badly of him. For imagining him capable of . . . what? I crumple inside, feel a sense of bitterest regret. As if something more of me had been expected in life, as if I should have known he couldn't see, should've known how to save my Freya's life.

I look out to where the horizon blurs into water, to where the last streaks of sunset are dissolving in the pinkest of skies.

'Close your eyes and listen. It will help you let go of this burden of yours.'

I'm too tired to argue, too tired to keep looking for some horizon my memory has wiped clean.

I shut my eyes, hear the sharp slap of waves down by the shoreline. And in between the thunderous claps, the trill of cicadas snaps the air; gulls' wings beat somewhere high above.

'Your path has brought you here,' the old man whispers. 'To where the ocean feeds the dank lagoon waters. A place for renewal, a chance to let go of grief, but only if you have the mind to listen.'

With each spoken word I feel something ease, a loosening of knots.

Around me I hear the faint rustle of acacia pods, no louder than the flight of a dragonfly. I listen deeper, to the shush of sand and beat of my own heart, as if each droplet of sound has been cut out and hung on the wind that now blows off the ocean. The humid sigh of breeze touches my face; I sigh back.

All at once a chord strikes low and mellow, like the string of a bass or the velvet hum of Freya's voice that first day we met. Then a lighter sound wings its way through the air, a birdsong, or is it the echo of her laughter? Suddenly her face clears in my head, that dimpled smile, eyes shining blue. My arms are wrapped around her as if I'll never let go.

More notes strum the air, dulcet tones in harmonic succession, as lucid now as the years we spent together; sweeter-sounding than anything I've heard before. A song of memories weaving its chords high above all the others, filling the empty spaces inside me, letting me remember.

A huge laugh breaks through it all, my own sound, one from long ago as I realize what the old man was speaking of, this song of the air, this melody of ocean.

Life finally calling me back again.

*Monica Watson-Peck*

Printed in the United Kingdom
by Lightning Source UK Ltd.
107532UKS00002B/85-207